Arnold Wesker

Roots

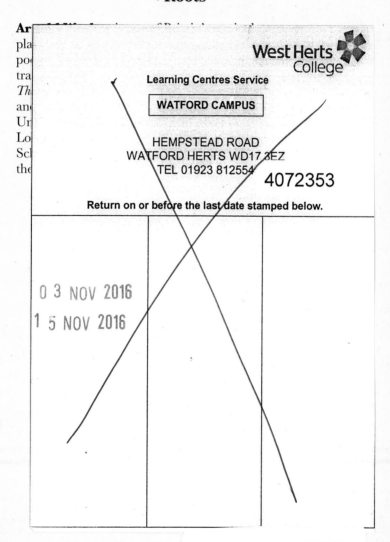

Arnold Wesker

Roots

B L O O M S B U R Y
LONDON • NEW DELHI • NEW YORK • SYDNEY

Bloomsbury Methuen Drama

An imprint of Bloomsbury Publishing Plc

50 Bedford Square	1385 Broadway
London	New York
WC1B 3DP	NY 10018
UK	USA

www.bloomsbury.com

Bloomsbury is a registered trade mark of Bloomsbury Publishing Plc

First published 1959

First published by Methuen Drama in 2001 as part of *Wesker Plays 1*
Published in 2008 as part of *The Methuen Drama Book of Plays from the Sixties*
Published in 2013 in this edition with a new cover and introductory material

British Library Cataloguing-in-Publication Data
A catalogue record for this book is available from the British Library.

Library of Congress Cataloging-in-Publication Data
A catalog record for this book is available from the Library of Congress.

ISBN: PB: 978-1-4725-2771-4
ePub: 978-1-4725-2245-0
ePDF: 978-1-4725-3157-5

Typeset by Country Setting, Kingsdown, Kent CT14 8ES
Printed and bound in Great Britain

Introduction

It was *Roots* that was voted on to the National Theatre's list of the hundred most important twentieth-century English-language plays, and which represents Arnold Wesker's work there, rather than the equally well-known *The Kitchen* or *Chips with Everything*. As well as being a favourite among Wesker's works, *Roots* (1959) is a seminal play in the British new wave of realist, socially aware drama of the fifties and sixties. At that time, the themes and settings of these plays – social division, youthful challenges to apathy, distinctive regional lifestyles and speech patterns, the foregrounding of ordinary routine – made a strong impact on audiences. *Roots* itself is a many-layered play. The second play of a trilogy, it moves away from the political idealists and activists of the other two plays, *Chicken Soup with Barley* and *I'm Talking about Jerusalem*, to focus on the low-paid agricultural workers of Norfolk. It not only shows us the life problems and humour of struggling farm labourers, it also penetrates to the underlying social unfairness that paralyses them, just as John Osborne's *Look Back in Anger* attacked the immovability of the Establishment and John Arden's *Serjeant Musgrave's Dance* dramatised the destructiveness of violent protest. But in spite of some outrage and bewilderment among traditionalists, audiences were intrigued by these plays, and although Wesker has become known for his confrontations with reviewers, from the first *Roots* gained critical recognition, as in Bernard Levin's claim that 'I have now seen this great and shining play three times and it seems to have grown visibly in stature each time' (*Daily Express*, 20 June 1959).

Of course, this does not mean that the elements of the new wave were totally unfamiliar, in spite of the mythology that London theatres had previously produced only light comedies and thrillers. Most decades of the twentieth century probably could show a regional or socially rebellious play or two, either by British writers such as Galsworthy or by European or American dramatists from Gorky to Odets. Yet somehow the context in the late fifties and early sixties seemed to be different. Post-war Britain was changing, and rather than plays addressing single issues in isolation there was a feeling that more change was needed, everywhere, faster. Similarly, there had always been working-class, regional activists who identified with their local culture and did not wish to be absorbed into the Establishment, but now there were far more and they could recognise themselves in plays which addressed their concerns.

Roots, then, was central to a movement in theatre that partly stemmed from new social pressures in the fifties and was partly fostered by specific theatrical cultures, such as that of the Royal Court Theatre, where Wesker among other young playwrights took part in workshops and discussions. Clearly *Roots* expresses the common concerns of the fifties and sixties younger generation – awareness of class divisions, economic exploitation, anti-colonialism, inadequacy of educational and health provisions, apathy among the exploited, censoriousness, anti-nuclear and anti-militaristic activism. Most of the issues associated with this period of great change can be detected either overtly or, often, gently slipped between the lines or behind a joke. Like his contemporaries, Wesker smacks at a range of abuses, then probes beneath to the basic cause of them – their roots, we might say – namely, the disconnection of the majority of the people from control of their own society.

So it is actually the characters' connections, or lack of them, to the society they live in which are the 'roots' of the title. This is not terribly obvious at first glance, and was not what audiences expected of a play set in rural Norfolk. Early critics found the implications of the title counterintuitive, and tried to wring a different kind of sense out of it. Reviewers wondered if the play meant that our roots needed to be grubbed up at once, or that a country girl can only escape her roots by staying in town. Yet the key idea of the play is the opposite of this: rootlessness applies to town and country alike, as the main character, Beatie Bryant, spells out in her climactic closing speech: 'Something's cut us off from the beginning. I'm telling you we've got no roots' (Act Three). The great majority have no roots in their own society, and are merely passengers,

partly from ignorance, partly from apathy, partly from a
feeling of disempowerment.

It is through the much-mentioned realism – or, as one critic
noted, 'old-fashioned naturalism', in the sense of strong
emphasis on the material conditions of daily life – that the
dislocation theme is developed. Beatie Bryant arrives back
from London to stay first with her married sister Jenny, then
with her mother and father. Jenny's primitive cottage, without
electricity or any other modern conveniences, is the background
to Beatie's confidences about her rocky relationship with her
London boyfriend Ronnie, and these confidences are
interspersed among scenes of eating and tidying up, often
lapsing into silence. As a stage direction in Act One explains:
'*this is a silence that needs organising. Throughout the play there is no sign
of intense living from any of the characters – Beatie's bursts are the
exception . . . The silences are important – as important as the way they
speak, if we are to know them.*' Beatie makes it clear to Jenny and
to the audience that Ronnie's lifestyle, as a political and social
radical, deeply involved in cultural activities, is profoundly
alien to the taciturn, slow-moving though affectionate
existence of Jenny's family.

The second act, set in Beatie's parents' cottage, which does
have electricity but has no bathroom, shows this again. Her
mother's slow ferrying in the water for the hip bath, Beatie's
making a cake, putting away the lunch things, emphasise for
us the texture of daily living. Mrs Bryant's repetitive dialogue
parallels the routine as she narrates well-worn exchanges with
neighbours – Beatie comments 'it's nearly always me listening
to you telling who's dead', and 'Do you know I've heard that
story a dozen times. A dozen times' (Act Two). Beatie
explicitly blames her mother for her limitations in this act, yet
the weight of Mrs Bryant's monotonous isolation surely
arouses our sympathy for her too. It is not usually noticed that
she maintains her resentful relationship with her husband not
for traditional or religious reasons, but because of economics:
she snaps, 'If I had a chance to be away working somewhere
the whole lot of you's could go to hell' (Act Three). The

economic strains on mean Mr Bryant are clear enough too – he stints his wife of housekeeping money (in the traditional way she doesn't even know how much he earns), but he in turn is kept under tight pressure by his boss, the farm manager, who comes round to check on his claim to be ill, and, as Beatie notes, under his smooth manner is issuing a threat.

So by the time the Bryant family assemble in the third act to await Ronnie's arrival, tension has built up in expectation of how this articulate and perhaps opinionated Londoner is going to interact with the defensive Norfolk folk. The afternoon begins badly with Mr Bryant revealing that he has been put on 'casual labour' by his manager, at half wages. The family's grim, defeated acceptance of this blow rejects Beatie's outrage: they won't discuss it; they never protest. This mirrors their reaction to the second and climactic blow of this act, when a letter arrives to tell Beatie that Ronnie has abruptly ended their relationship. Her hysterical despair is played against a background of resigned sympathy – it is assumed again that nothing can be done, in emotional as much as social terms. The exception is Mrs Bryant, who shocks her family and the audience by slapping Beatie's face in response to her daughter's accusations: complex emotions coexist with acquiescence. Beatie's key speech, which ends the play, repeats the theme – that she and her family are unable to interact with the world outside their narrow limits, because of their own unwillingness to even try to interact. Her own sudden realisation that she has in fact started to reason for herself is the fascinating dramatic reversal which enables the play to end on a fragile note of hope.

At this point, a question may arise in the audience's or reader's mind: is a girl in Beatie's situation, with all her problems, really likely to make a breakthrough to articulacy and perceptiveness about herself and the culture she is part of? Yet in spite of her self-criticism, the play shows her as open to new ideas. She parrots Ronnie's words, but she seems already to be making a start on applying them to Jimmy's territorials, to her father's work situation and to other incidents. She is intelligent and lively, and Ronnie's influence has given her the incentive to see connections and make parallels which are analytic. The fresh gaze she brings to her old home prompts new thoughts, and finally experience of rejection and hurt makes her look for answers beyond the immediate and personal.

This relates to a recurrent theme in Wesker's plays: self-discovery, in the form of the emergence of a new side of a character's personality. Beatie repeats Ronnie's mantra, initially formulated by his father in the earlier *Chicken Soup*, that 'you can't change people . . . you can only give them some love and hope they'll take it' (Act Two). Yet if people do take this love – or if they undergo some more unpleasant learning experience – it is possible for them to change themselves. Wesker's characters do this through self-discovery – finding hidden resources within themselves – and Beatie discovers that she has strengths she had previously ignored.

Both the style and the message of *Roots* have retained their importance into the new century. After *Roots*, the smell of onions or bacon floated over many auditoriums as other playwrights put real cooking on stage, and the naturalistic depiction of a slice of regional working-class life, for instance in the plays of David Storey, became a genre which was accepted without further critical indignation. *Roots* itself was not only successful in London, it was successful wherever it was put on. The central role was a desirable one for any actress, and reviews praise the leading ladies of provincial reps across the country for their triumphs as Beatie Bryant. In 1979 the play was revived at the National Theatre, and although the clothes and set were anchored in the fifties, it was noted that the attack on divisions in society were still valid. Today, after some delusional decades in which it was claimed that 'everybody's middle class now', it is clear that social division has increased rather than reduced, and the distance between those in power and those at the bottom is greater than ever. There may be wider provision of electricity and indoor plumbing, but the Bryant family's feeling of powerlessness is recognisable enough in the twenty-first century.

The value of Wesker's work relates in part to his perceptiveness about this situation. He is the longest surviving member of the new-wave dramatists of the fifties and sixties, and his best known plays of that period – *The Kitchen*, *Chicken Soup with Barley*, *Roots*, *Chips with Everything* – are not mere realistic vignettes of different mid-century lifestyles: all of them pinpoint the uncomfortable conflicts, the complicity, the lethargy, that enmesh the struggling lives of Wesker's marginalised fellow-citizens. Amongst other themes, *Roots* is a forerunner of some of Wesker's later, lesser known plays, such as *The Friends* and *Annie Wobbler*, in depicting the experiences of women characters. Conversely, the Jewish identity of offstage Ronnie and his family, central to the other parts of the trilogy, is hardly mentioned in *Roots* (Jimmy remarks 'a strong socialist . . . and a Jew boy? . . . Well, that's a queer mixture then' (Act Three)), but this identity is important to Wesker, whose reworking in his *Shylock* of Shakespeare's *The Merchant of Venice* has been and still is enormously popular with audiences and scholars across the world. Unlike his contemporaries Osborne and Arden, who wrote less as they grew older and met with persistent discouragement, Wesker has always continued to write, including for radio, television and local commissions. When he was awarded a knighthood in 2006, it was for services to drama, which particularly included his work in making London's Roundhouse into a theatrical venue, work which strongly influenced the development of arts centres opening up in cities across the country. Other contemporaries are known to have declined honours for ideological reasons, but Wesker considered the recognition was deserved. And he did deserve it.

Glenda Leeming, 2013

Roots

For Dusty

Note to actors and producers

My people are not caricatures. They are real (though fiction), and if they are portrayed as caricatures the point of all these plays will be lost. The picture I have drawn is a harsh one, yet my tone is not one of disgust – nor should it be in the presentation of the plays. I am at one with these people: it is only that I am annoyed, with them and myself.

Notes on pronunciation

This is a play about Norfolk people; it could be a play about any country people and the moral could certainly extend to the metropolis. But as it is about Norfolk people it is important that some attempt is made to find out how they talk. A very definite accent and intonation exists and personal experience suggests that this is not difficult to know. The following may be of great help:

When the word 'won't' is used, the 'w' is left out. It sounds the same but the 'w' is lost.

Double 'ee' is pronounced 'i' as in 'it' – so that 'been' becomes 'bin', 'seen' becomes 'sin', etc.

'Have' and 'had' become 'hev' and 'hed' as in 'head'.

'Ing' loses the 'g' so that it becomes 'in'.

'Bor' is a common handle and is a contraction of neighbour.

Instead of the word 'of' they say 'on', e.g. 'I've hed enough on it' or 'What do you think on it?'

Their 'yes' is used all the time and sounds like 'year' with a 'p' – 'yearp'.

'Blast' is also common usage and is pronounced 'blust', a short sharp sound as in 'gust'.

The cockney 'ain't' becomes 'ent' – also short and sharp.

The 't' in 'that' and 'what' is left out to give 'thaas' and 'whaas', e.g. 'Whaas matter then?'

Other idiosyncrasies are indicated in the play itself.

Roots was first presented at the Belgrade Theatre, Coventry, on 25 May 1959, with the following cast:

Jenny Beales	Patsy Byrne
Jimmy Beales	Charles Kay
Beatie Bryant	Joan Plowright
Stan Mann	Patrick O'Connell
Mrs Bryant	Gwen Nelson
Mr Bryant	Jack Rodney
Mr Healey	Richard Martin
Frankie Bryant	Alan Howard
Pearl Bryant	Brenda Peters

Directed by John Dexter
Designed by Jocelyn Herbert

The play transferred to the Royal Court Theatre, London, on 30 June 1959, and subsequently to the Duke of York's Theatre on 30 July 1959. At the Duke of York's the part of Mr Healey was played by Barry Wilsher.

Roots was revived at the Donmar Warehouse, London, on 3 October 2013, and featured the following cast and creatives.

Jenny	Lisa Ellis
Jimmy	Michael Jibson
Beatie	Jessica Raine
Stan Mann	David Burke
Mrs Bryant	Linda Bassett
Mr Bryant	Ian Gelder
Mr Healey	Nic Jackman
Frank Bryant	Carl Prekopp
Pearl	Emma Stansfield

Director James Macdonald
Designer Hildegard Bechtler
Lighting Designer Guy Hoare
Sound Designer Ian Dickinson for Autograph
Video Designer Dick Straker
Casting Director Alastair Coomer CDG

Characters

Beatie Bryant, *a young woman aged twenty-two, a friend of Ronnie Kahn*
Jenny Beales, *her sister*
Jimmy Beales, *her brother-in-law*
Mrs Bryant, *her mother*
Mr Bryant, *her father*
Frankie Bryant, *her brother*
Pearl Bryant, *her sister-in-law*
Stan Mann, *a neighbour of the Beales*
Mr Healey, *a manager at the farm*

Act One   *An isolated cottage in Norfolk, the house of the Beales*

Act Two, Scene One   *Two days later at the cottage of Mr and Mrs Bryant, in the kitchen*

Act Two, Scene Two   *The same a couple of hours later*

Act Three   *Two weeks later in the front room of the Bryants*

Time: 1958

Act One

A rather ramshackle house in Norfolk where there is no water laid on, nor electricity, nor gas. Everything rambles and the furniture is cheap and old. If it is untidy it is because there is a child in the house and there are few amenities, so that the mother is too overworked to take much care.

An assortment of clobber lies around: papers and washing, coats and basins, a tin wash-tub with shirts and underwear to be cleaned, Tilley lamps and Primus stoves. Washing hangs on a line in the room. It is September.

Jenny Beales *is by the sink washing up. She is singing a recent pop song. She is short, fat and friendly, and wears glasses. A child's voice is heard from the bedroom crying 'Sweet, Mamma, sweet.'*

Jenny (*good-naturedly*) Shut you up Daphne and get you to sleep now. (*Moves to get a dishcloth.*)

Child's voice Daphy wan' sweet, sweet, sweet.

Jenny (*going to cupboard to get sweet*) My word child, Father come home and find you awake he'll be after you. (*Disappears to bedroom with sweet.*) There – now sleep, gal, don't wan' you grumpy wi' me in the mornin'.

Enter **Jimmy Beales**. *Also short, chubby, blond though hardly any hair left, ruddy complexion. He is a garage mechanic. Wears blue dungarees and an army pack slung over his shoulder. He wheels his bike in and lays it by the wall. Seems to be in some sort of pain – around his back.* **Jenny** *returns.*

Waas matter wi' you then?

Jimmy I don' know gal. There's a pain in my guts and one a'tween my shoulder blades I can hardly stand up.

Jenny Sit you down then an' I'll git you your supper on the table.

Jimmy Blust gal! I can't eat yit.

Jimmy *picks up a pillow from somewhere and lies down on the sofa holding pillow to stomach.* **Jenny** *watches him a while.*

Jenny   Don't you know what 'tis yit?

Jimmy   Well, how should *I* know what 'tis.

Jenny   I told Mother about the pain and she says it's indigestion.

Jimmy   What the hell's indigestion doin' a'tween my shoulder blades then?

Jenny   She say some people get indigestion so bad it go right through their stomach to the back.

Jimmy   Don't be daft.

Jenny   That's what I say. Blust Mother, I say, you don't git indigestion in the back. Don't you tell me, she say, I hed it!

Jimmy   What hevn't she hed.

Jenny *returns to washing up while* **Jimmy** *struggles a while on the sofa.* **Jenny** *hums. No word. Then –*

Jenny   Who d'you see today?

Jimmy   Only Doctor Gallagher.

Jenny *(wheeling round)*   You see who?

Jimmy   Gallagher. His wife driv him up in the ole Armstrong.

Jenny   Well I go t'hell if that ent a rum thing.

Jimmy *(rising and going to table; pain has eased)*   What's that then?

Jenny *(moving to get him supper from oven)*   We was down at the whist drive in the village and that Judy Maitland say he were dead. 'Cos you know he've hed a cancer this last year and they don't give him no longer'n three weeks don't you?

Jimmy   Ole crows. They don' wan' nothin' less than a death to wake them up.

Jenny   No. No longer'n three weeks.

Girl's voice (*off*)   Yoo-hoo! Yoo-hoo!

Jimmy   There's your sister.

Jenny   That's her.

Girl's voice (*off*)   Yoo-hoo! Anyone home?

Jenny (*calling*)   Come you on in gal, don't you worry about yoo-hoo.

Enter **Beatie Bryant**, *an ample, blonde, healthy-faced young woman of twenty-two years. She is carrying a case.*

Jimmy   Here she is.

Jenny (*with reserve, but pleased*)   Hello, Beatrice – how are you?

Beatie (*with reserve, but pleased*)   Hello, Jenny – how are you? What's that lovely smell I smell?

Jenny   Onions for supper and bread for the harvest festival.

Beatie   Watcha Jimmy Beales, how you doin' bor?

Jimmy   Not so bad gal, how's yourself?

Beatie   All right you know. When you comin' to London again for a football match?

Jimmy   O blust gal, I don' wanna go to any more o' those things. Ole father Bryant was there in the middle of that crowd and he turn around an' he say (*imitating*), 'Stop you a-pushin' there,' he say, 'stop you a-pushin'.'

Jenny   Where's Ronnie?

Beatie   He's comin' down at the end of two weeks.

Jimmy   Ent you married yit?

Beatie   No.

Jimmy   You wanna hurry then gal, a long engagement don't do the ole legs any good.

Jenny   Now shut you up Jimmy Beales and get that food down you. Every time you talk, look, you miss a mouthful! That's why you complain of pain in your shoulder blades.

Beatie   You bin hevin' pains then Jimmy?

Jimmy   Blust yes! Right a'tween my shoulder blades.

Jenny   Mother says it's indigestion.

Beatie   What the hell's indigestion doin' a'tween his shoulder blades?

Jenny   Mother reckon some people get indigestion so bad it go right through their stomach to the back.

Beatie   Don't talk daft!

Jenny   That's what I say. Blust Mother, I say, you don't git indigestion in the back. Don't you tell me, she say, I hed it!

Beatie   What hevn't she hed. How is she?

Jenny   Still the same you know. How long you staying this time?

Beatie   Two days here – two weeks at home.

Jenny   Hungry gal?

Beatie   Watcha got?

Jenny   Watcha see.

Beatie   Liver? I'll hev it!

Beatie *makes herself at home. Nearby is a pile of comics. She picks one up and reads.*

Jenny   We got some ice cream after.

Beatie (*absorbed*)   Yearp.

Jenny   Look at her. No sooner she's in than she's at them ole comics. You still read them ole things?

Jimmy   She don't change much do she?

Beatie   Funny that! Soon ever I'm home again I'm like I always was – it don' even seem I bin away. I do the same lazy things an' I talk the same. Funny that!

Jenny   What do Ronnie say to it?

Beatie   He ent never bin here, not in the three years I know him so he don't even know. But I'll tell you. (*She jumps up and moves around as she talks.*) I used to read the comics he bought for his nephews and he used to get riled –

Now **Beatie** *begins to quote Ronnie, and when she does she imitates him so well in both manner and intonation that in fact as the play progresses we see a picture of him through her.*

'Christ, woman, what can they give you that you can *be* so absorbed?' So you know what I used to do? I used to get a copy of the *Manchester Guardian* and sit with that wide open – and a comic behind!

Jimmy   *Manchester Guardian*? Blimey Joe – he don' believe in hevin' much fun then?

Beatie   That's what I used to tell him. 'Fun?' he say. 'Fun? Playing an instrument is fun, painting is fun, reading a book is fun, talking with friends is fun – but a comic? A comic? for a young woman of twenty-two?'

Jenny (*handing out meal and sitting down herself*)   He sound a queer bor to me. Sit you down and eat gal.

Beatie (*enthusiastically*)   He's alive though.

Jimmy   Alive? Alive you say? What's alive about someone who can't read a comic? What's alive about a person that reads books and looks at paintings and listens to classical music?

There is a silence at this, as though the question answers itself – reluctantly.

Well, it's all right for some I suppose.

Beatie   And then he'd sneak the comic away from me and read it his-self!

Jenny   Oh, he didn't really mind then?

Beatie   No – 'cos sometimes I read books as well. 'There's nothing wrong with comics,' he'd cry – he stand up on a chair when he want to preach but don't wanna sound too dramatic.

Jimmy   Eh?

Beatie   Like this, look. (*Stands on a chair.*) 'There's nothing wrong with comics only there's something wrong with comics all the time. There's nothing wrong with football, only there's something wrong with *only* football. There's nothing wrong with rock 'n' rolling, only God preserve me from the girl that can do nothing else!' (*She sits down and then stands up again, remembering something else.*) Oh yes, 'and there's nothing wrong with talking about the weather, only don't talk to me about it!' (*Sits down.*)

Jimmy *and* **Jenny** *look at each other as though she, and no doubt Ronnie, is a little barmy.* **Jimmy** *rises and begins to strap on boots and gaiters ready for going out to an allotment.*

Jenny   He never really row with you then?

Beatie   We used to. There was a time when he handled all official things for me you know. Once I was in between jobs and I didn't think to ask for my unemployment benefit. *He* told me to. But when I asked they told me I was short on stamps and so I wasn't entitled to benefit. *I* didn't know what to say but he did. He went up and argued for me – he's just like his mother, she argues with everyone – and I got it. I didn't know how to talk see, it was all foreign to me. Think of it! An English girl born and bred and I couldn't talk the language – except for to buy food and clothes. And so sometimes when he were in a black mood he'd start on me. 'What can you talk of?' he'd ask. 'Go on, pick a subject. Talk. Use the language. Do you know what language is?' Well, I'd never thought before – hev you? – it's automatic to you isn't it, like walking? 'Well, language is words,' he'd say, as though he were telling me a secret. 'It's bridges, so that you can get safely from one place to another. And the more bridges you know about the more places you can see!' (*To* **Jimmy**.) And do *you* know what happens when you can see a place but you don't know where the bridge is?

Jimmy (*angrily*)   Blust gal, what the hell are you on about.

Beatie   Exactly! You see, you hev a row! Still, rows is all right. I like a row. So then he'd say: 'Bridges! bridges! bridges! Use your bridges woman. It took thousands of years to build them, use them!' And that riled me. 'Blust your bridges,' I'd say. 'Blust you and your bridges – I want a row.' Then he'd grin at me. 'You want a row?' he'd ask. 'No bridges this time?' 'No bridges,' I'd say – and we'd row. Sometimes he hurt me but then, slowly, he'd build the bridge up *for* me – and then we'd make love! (*Innocently continues her meal.*)

Jenny   You'd what, did you say?

Beatie   Make love. Love in the afternoon gal. Ever had it? It's the only time *for* it. Go out or entertain in the evenings; sleep at night, study, work and chores in the mornings; but love – alert and fresh, when you got most energy – love in the afternoon.

Jimmy   I suppose you take time off from work every afternoon to do it?

Beatie   I'm talking about weekends and holidays – daft.

Jenny   Oh, Beatie, go on wi' you!

Beatie   Well, go t'hell Jenny Beales, you're blushin'. Ent you never had love in the afternoon? Ask Jimmy then.

Jenny (*rising to get sweet*)   Shut you up gal and get on wi' your ice cream. It's strawberry flavour. Want some more James?

Jimmy (*taking it in the middle of lacing up boots*)   Yes please, vanilla please. (*Eating.*) Good cream ent it? Made from the white milk of a Jersey cow.

Beatie   This is good too – made from pink milk ent it?

Pause.

Jimmy   Yearp! (*Pause.*) Come from a pink cow!

Pause. They are all enjoying the cream.

Jenny (*eating*)   You remember Dickie Smart, Beatie?

Beatie (*eating*)   Who?

Jenny (*eating*)   We had a drink wi' him in the Storks when you was down last.

Beatie (*eating*)   Yearp.

Jenny (*eating*)   Well, he got gored by a bull last Thursday. His left ear was nearly off, his knee were gored, his ribs bruised, and the ligaments of his legs torn.

Pause as they finish eating.

Beatie (*euphemistically*)   He had a rough time then!

Jenny   Yearp. (*To* **Jimmy**.) You off now?

Jimmy   Mm.

Jenny *collects dishes.*

Beatie   Still got your allotment Jimmy?

Jimmy   Yearp.

Beatie   Bit heavy-going this weather.

Jimmy   That ent too bad just yit – few more weeks an' the old mowld'll cling.

Beatie   Watcha got this year?

Jimmy   Had spuds, carrots, cabbages, you know. Beetroot, lettuces, onions, and peas. But me runners let me down this year though.

Jenny   I don't go much on them old things.

Beatie   You got a fair owle turn then?

Jimmy   Yearp.

Jimmy *starts to sharpen a reap hook.*

Beatie (*jumping up*)   I'll help you wash.

Jenny   That's all right gal.

Beatie   Where's the cloth?

Jenny   Here 'tis.

Beatie *helps collect dishes from table and proceeds to help wash up. This is a silence that needs organising. Throughout the play there is no sign of intense living from any of the characters –* **Beatie**'s *bursts are the exception. They continue in a routine rural manner. The day comes, one sleeps at night, there is always the winter, the spring, the autumn, and the summer – little amazes them. They talk in fits and starts mainly as a sort of gossip, and they talk quickly too, enacting as though for an audience what they say. Their sense of humour is keen and dry. They show no affection for each other – though this does not mean they would not be upset were one of them to die. The silences are important – as important as the way they speak, if we are to know them.*

Jenny   What about that strike in London? Waas London like wi'out the buses?

Beatie   Lovely! No noise – and the streets, you should see the streets, flowing with people – the city looks human.

Jimmy   They wanna call us Territorials out – we'd soon break the strike.

Beatie   That's a soft thing for a worker to say for his mates.

Jimmy   Soft be buggered, soft you say? What they earnin' those busmen, what they earnin'? And what's the farm worker's wage? Do you know it gal?

Beatie   Well, let the farm workers go on strike too then! It don't help a farm labourer if a busman don't go on strike do it now?

Jenny   You know they've got a rise though. Father Bryant's go up by six and six a week as a pigman, and Frank goes up seven 'n' six a week for driving a tractor.

Jimmy   But you watch the Hall sack some on 'em.

Jenny   Thaas true Beatie. They're such sods, honest to God they are. Every time there's bin a rise someone gets sacked. Without fail. You watch it – you ask father Bryant when you get home, ask him who's bin sacked since the rise.

Beatie   One person they 'ont sack is him though. They 'ont find many men'd tend to pigs seven days a week and stay up the hours he do.

Jenny   Bloody fool! (*Pause.*) Did Jimmy tell you he've bin chosen for the Territorials' Jubilee in London this year?

Beatie   What's this then? What'll you do there?

Jimmy   Demonstrate and parade wi' arms and such like.

Beatie   Won't do you any good.

Jimmy   Don't you reckon? Gotta show we can defend the country you know. Demonstrate arms and you prevent war.

Beatie (*she has finished wiping up*)   Won't demonstrate anything bor. (*Goes to undo her case.*) Present for the house! Have a hydrogen bomb fall on you and you'll find them things silly in your hands. (*Searches for other parcels.*)

Jimmy   So you say gal? So you say? That'll frighten them other buggers though.

Beatie   Frighten yourself y'mean. (*Finds parcels.*) Presents for the kid.

Jimmy   And what do you know about this all of a sudden?

Jenny (*revealing a tablecloth*)   Thank you very much Beatie. Just what I need.

Beatie   You're not interested in defending your country Jimmy, you just enjoy playing soldiers.

Jimmy   What did I do in the last war then – *sing* in the trenches?

Beatie (*explaining – not trying to get one over on him*)   Ever heard of Chaucer, Jimmy?

Jimmy   No.

Beatie   Do you know the MP for this constituency?

Jimmy   What you drivin' at gal – don't give me no riddles.

Beatie   Do you know how the British Trade Union Movement started? And do you believe in strike action?

Jimmy   No to both those.

Beatie   What you goin' to war to defend then?

Jimmy (*he is annoyed now*)   Beatie – you bin away from us a long time now – you got a boy who's educated an' that and he's taught you a lot maybe. But don't you come pushin' ideas across at us – we're all right as we are. You can come when you like an' welcome but don't bring no discussion of politics in the house wi' you 'cos that'll only cause trouble. I'm telling you. (*He goes off.*)

Jenny   Blust gal, if you hevn't touched him on a sore spot. He live for them Territorials he do – that's half his life.

Beatie (*she is upset now*)   What's he afraid of talking for?

Jenny   He ent afraid of talking Beatie – blust he can do that, gal.

Beatie   But not talk, not really talk, not use bridges. I sit with Ronnie and his friends sometimes and I listen to them talk about things and you know I've never heard half of the words before.

Jenny   Don't he tell you what they mean?

Beatie   I get annoyed when he keep tellin' me – and he want me to ask. (*Imitates him half-heartedly now.*) 'Always ask, people love to tell you what they know, always ask and people will respect you.'

Jenny   And do you?

Beatie   No! I don't! An' you know why? Because I'm stubborn, I'm like Mother, I'm stubborn. Somehow I just can't

bring myself to ask, and you know what? I go mad when I
listen to them. As soon as they start to talk about things I don't
know about or I can't understand I get mad. They sit there,
casually talking, and suddenly they turn on you, abrupt. 'Don't
you think?' they say. Like at school, pick on you and ask a
question you ent ready for. Sometimes I don't say anything,
sometimes I go to bed or leave the room. Like Jimmy – just
like Jimmy.

Jenny   And what do Ronnie say to that then?

Beatie   He get mad too. 'Why don't you ask me woman, for
God's sake why don't you ask me? Aren't I dying to tell you
about things? Only ask!'

Jenny   And he's goin' to marry you?

Beatie   Why not?

Jenny   Well I'm sorry gal, you mustn't mind me saying this,
but it don't seem to me like you two got much in common.

Beatie (*loudly*)   It's not true! We're in love!

Jenny   Well, you know.

Beatie (*softly*)   No, I don't know. I won't know till he come
here. From the first day I went to work as waitress in the Dell
Hotel and saw him working in the kitchen I fell in love – and
I thought it was easy. I thought everything was easy. I chased
him for three months with compliments and presents until I
finally give myself to him. He never said he love me nor I
didn't care but once he'd taken me he seemed to think he was
responsible for me and I told him no different. I'd *make* him
love me I thought. I didn't know much about him except he
was different and used to write most of the time. And then he
went back to London and I followed him there. I've never
moved far from home but I did for him and he felt all the time
he couldn't leave me and I didn't tell him no different. And
then I got to know more about him. He was interested in all
the things I never even thought about. About politics and art
and all that, and he tried to teach me. He's a socialist and he

used to say you couldn't bring socialism to a country by making speeches, but perhaps you could pass it on to someone who was near you. So I pretended I was interested – but I didn't understand much. All the time he's trying to teach me but I can't take it Jenny. And yet, at the same time, I want to show I'm willing. I'm not used to learning. Learning was at school and that's finished with.

Jenny   Blust gal, you don't seem like you're going to be happy then. Like I said.

Beatie   But I love him.

Jenny   Then you're not right in the head then.

Beatie   I couldn't have any other life now.

Jenny   Well, I don't know and that's a fact.

Beatie (*playfully mocking her*)   Well I don't know and that's a fact! (*Suddenly.*) Come on gal, I'll teach you how to bake some pastries.

Jenny   Pastries?

Beatie   Ronnie taught me.

Jenny   Oh, you learnt that much then?

Beatie   But he don't know. I always got annoyed when he tried to teach me to cook as well – Christ! I had to know something – but it sank in all the same.

By this time it has become quite dark and **Jenny** *proceeds to light a Tilley lamp.*

Jenny   You didn't make it easy then?

Beatie   Oh don't you worry, gal, it'll be all right once we're married. Once we're married and I got babies I won't need to be interested in half the things I got to be interested in now.

Jenny   No you won't will you! Don't need no education for babies.

Beatie   Nope. Babies is babies – you just have 'em.

Jenny   Little sods!

Beatie   You gonna hev another Jenny?

Jenny   Well, course I am. What you on about? Think Jimmy don't want none of his own?

Beatie   He's a good man Jenny.

Jenny   Yearp.

Beatie   Not many men'd marry you after you had a baby.

Jenny   No.

Beatie   He didn't ask you any questions? Who was the father? Nor nothing?

Jenny   No.

Beatie   You hevn't told no one hev you Jenny?

Jenny   No, that I hevn't.

Beatie   Well, that's it gal, don't you tell me then!

By this time the methylated spirit torch has burned out and **Jenny** *has finished pumping the Tilley lamp and we are in brightness.*

Jenny (*severely*)   Now Beatie, stop it. Every time you come home you ask me that question and I hed enough. It's finished with and over. No one don't say nothing and no one know. You hear me?

Beatie   Are you in love with Jimmy?

Jenny   Love? I don't believe in any of that squit – we just got married, an' that's that.

Beatie (*suddenly looking around the room at the general chaos*)   Jenny Beales, just look at this house. Look at it!

Jenny   I'm looking. What's wrong?

Beatie   Let's clean it up.

Jenny   Clean what up?

Beatie   Are you going to live in this house all your life?

Jenny   You gonna buy us another?

Beatie   Stuck out here in the wilds with only ole Stan Mann and his missus as a neighbour and sand pits all around. Every time it rain look you're stranded.

Jenny   Jimmy don't earn enough for much more 'n we got.

Beatie   But it's so untidy.

Jenny   You don' wan' me bein' like sister Susan do you? 'Cos you know how clean she is don' you – she's so bloody fussy she's gotten to polishing the brass overflow pipe what leads out from the lavatory.

Beatie   Come on gal, let's make some order anyway – I love tidying up.

Jenny   What about the pastries? Pastries? Oh my sainted aunt, the bread! (*Dashes to the oven and brings out a most beautiful-looking plaited loaf of bread. Admiring it.*) Well, no one wanna complain after that. Isn't that beautiful Beatie?

Beatie   I could eat it now.

Jenny   You hungry again?

Beatie (*making an attack upon the clothes that are lying around*)   I'm always hungry again. Ronnie say I eat more'n I need. 'If you get fat woman I'll leave you – without even a discussion!'

Jenny (*placing bread on large oval plate to put away*)   Well, there ent nothin' wrong in bein' fat.

Beatie   You ent got no choice gal. (*Seeing bike.*) A bike! What's a bike doin' in a livin' room – I'm putting it outside.

Jenny   Jimmy 'ont know where it is.

Beatie   Don't be daft, you can't miss a bike. (*Wheels it outside and calls from there.*) Jenny! Start puttin' the clothes away.

Jenny   Blust gal, I ent got nowhere to put them.

Beatie (*from outside*)   You got drawers – you got cupboards.

Jenny   They're full already.

Beatie (*entering – energy sparks from her*)   Come here – let's look. (*Looks.*) Oh, go away – you got enough room for ten families. You just bung it all in with no order, that's why. Here – help me.

They drag out all manner of clothes from the cupboard and begin to fold them up.

How's my Frankie and Pearl?

Jenny   They're all right. You know she and Mother don't talk to each other?

Beatie   What, again? Who's fault is it this time?

Jenny   Well, Mother she say it's Pearl's fault and Pearl she say it's Mother.

Beatie   Well, they wanna get together quick and find whose fault 'tis 'cos I'm going to call the whole family together for tea to meet Ronnie.

Jenny   Well, Susan and Mother don't talk neither so you got a lot of peace-making to do.

Beatie   Well go t'hell, what's broken them two up?

Jenny   Susan hev never bin stuck on her mother, you know that don't you – well, it seems that Susan bought something off the club from Pearl and Pearl give it to Mother and Mother sent it to Susan through the fishmonger what live next door her in the council houses. And of course Susan were riled 'cos she didn't want her neighbours to know that she bought anything off the club. So they don't speak.

Beatie   Kids! It makes me mad.

Jenny   And you know what 'tis with Pearl don't you – it's
'cos Mother hev never thought she was good enough for her
son Frankie.

Beatie   No more she wasn't neither!

Jenny   What's wrong wi' her then? I get on all right.

Beatie   Nothing's wrong wi' her, she just wasn't good
enough for our Frankie, that's all.

Jenny   Who's being small-minded now?

Beatie   Always wantin' more'n he can give her.

Jenny   An' I know someone else who always wanted more'n
she got.

Beatie (*sulkily*)   It's not the same thing.

Jenny   Oh yes 'tis.

Beatie   'Tent.

Jenny   'Tis my gal. (*Mimicking the child* **Beatie**.) I wan' a
'nana, a 'nana, a 'nana. Frankie's got my 'nana, 'nana, 'nana.

Beatie   Well, I liked bananas.

Jenny   You liked anything you could get your hands on and
Mother used to give in to you 'cos you were the youngest. Me
and Susan and Frankie never got nothing 'cos o' you – 'cept a
clout round the ear.

Beatie   'Tent so likely. You got everything and I got nothing.

Jenny   All we got was what we pinched out the larder and
then you used to go and tell tales to Mother.

Beatie   I never did.

Jenny   Oh, didn't you my gal? Many's the time I'd've
willingly strangled you – with no prayers – there you are, no
prayers whatsoever. Strangled you till you was dead.

Beatie   Oh go on wi' you Jenny Beales.

By now they have finished folding the clothes and have put away most of the laundry and garments that have till this moment cluttered up the room. **Beatie** *says 'There', stands up and looks around, finds some coats sprawled helter-skelter, and hangs them up behind the door.*

I'll buy you some coat-hangers.

Jenny   You get me a couple o' coats to hang on 'em first please.

Beatie (*looking around*)   What next. Bottles, jars, nicknacks, saucepans, cups, papers – everything anywhere. Look at it! Come on!

Beatie *attempts to get these things either into their proper places or out of sight.*

Jenny   You hit this place like a bloody whirlwind you do, like a bloody whirlwind. Jimmy'll think he've come into the wrong house and I shan't be able to find a thing.

Beatie   Here, grab a broom. (*She is now gurgling with sort of animal noises signifying excitement. Her joy is childlike.*) How's Poppy?

Jenny   Tight as ever.

Beatie   What won't he give you now?

Jenny   'Tent nothing wi' me gal. Nothing he do don't affect me. It's Mother I'm referring to.

Beatie   Don't he still give her much money?

Jenny   Money? She hev to struggle and skint all the time – *all* the time. Well it ent never bin no different from when we was kids hev it?

Beatie   No.

Jenny   I tell you what. It wouldn't surprise me if Mother were in debt all the time, that it wouldn't. No. It wouldn't surprise me at all.

Beatie   Oh, never.

Jenny   Well, what do you say that for Beatie – do you know how much he allow her a week look?

Beatie   Six pounds?

Jenny   Six pound be buggered. Four pounds ten! An' she hev to keep house *an'* buy her own clothes out of that.

Beatie   Still, there's only two on 'em.

Jenny   You try keepin' two people in food for four pound ten. She pay seven an' six a week into Pearl's club for clothes, two and six she hev on the pools, and a shilling a week on the Labour Tote. (*Suddenly.*) Blust! I forgot to say. Pearl won the Tote last week.

Beatie   A hundred pounds?

Jenny   A hundred pounds!

Beatie   Well no one wrote me about it.

Jenny   'Cos you never wrote no one else.

Beatie   What she gonna do wi' it – buy a TV?

Jenny   TV? Blust no. You know she hevn't got electricity in that house. No, she say she's gonna get some clothes for the kids.

There is a sound now of a drunk old man approaching, and alongside of it the voice of **Jimmy***. The drunk is singing: 'I come from Bungay Town, I calls I Bungay Johnnie.'*

Well I go t'hell if that ent Stan Mann drunk again. And is that Jimmy wi' him? (*Listens.*)

Beatie   But I thought Stan Mann was paralysed.

Jenny   That don't stop him getting paralytic drunk. (*Listens again.*) That's Jimmy taking him into the house I bet. A fortune that man hev drunk away – a whole bleedin' fortune. Remember the fleet of cars he used to run and all that land he owned, and all them cattle he had and them fowl? Well, he've only got a few acres left and a few ole chickens. He drink it all away. Two

strokes he've had from drinking and now he's paralysed down
one side. But that don't stop him getting drunk – no it don't.

Jimmy *enters and throws his jacket on the couch, takes off his boots and
gaiters, and smiles meanwhile.*

Jimmy   Silly ole bugger.

Jenny   I was just telling Beatie how he've drunk a fortune
away hevn't he?

Jimmy   He wanna drink a little more often and he'll be
finished for good.

Jenny   Didn't he hev all them cows and cars and land
Jimmy? And didn't he drink it all away bit by bit?

Jimmy   Silly ole sod don't know when to stop.

Jenny   I wished I had half the money he drink.

Jimmy   He messed his pants.

Jenny   He what? Well where was this then?

Jimmy   By the allotment.

Jenny   Well, what did *you* do then?

Jimmy   He come up to me – 'course I knowed he were
drunk the way he walk – he come up to me an' he say,
''Evenin' Jimmy Beales, thaas a fine turnover you got there.'
An' I say, 'Yearp 'tis.' An' then he bend down to pick a carrot
from the ground an' then he cry, 'Oops, I done it again!' An'
'course, soon ever he say 'done it again' I knowed what'd
happened. So I took his trousers down an' ran the ole hose
over him.

Beatie   Oh, Jimmy, you never did.

Jimmy   I did gal. I put the ole hose over him an' brought
him home along the fields with an ole sack around his waist.

Beatie   He'll catch his death.

Jimmy   Never – he's strong as an ox.

Jenny   What'd you do with his trousers and things?

Jimmy   Put it on the compost heap – good for the land!

Now **Stan Mann** *enters. He's not all that drunk. The cold water has sobered him a little. He is old – about seventy-five – and despite his slight stoop one can see he was a very strong upright man. He probably looks like every man's idea of a farmer – except that he wears no socks or boots at this moment and he hobbles on a stick.*

Stan   Sorry about that ole son.

Jimmy   Don't you go worrying about that my manny – get you along to bed.

Jenny   Get some shoes on you too Stan, or you'll die of cold *and* booze.

Stan (*screwing up his eyes across the room*)   Is that you Jenny? Hello ole gal. How are you?

Jenny   It's you you wanna worry about now ole matey. I'm well enough.

Stan (*screwing his eyes still more*)   Who's that next to you?

Jenny   Don't you recognise her? It's our Beatie, Stan.

Stan   Is that you Beatie? Well blust gal, you gotten fatter since I seen you last. You gonna be fat as Jenny here? Come on over an' let's look at you.

Beatie (*approaching*)   Hello Stan Mann, how are you?

Stan (*looking her up and down*)   Well enough gal, well enough. You married yit?

Beatie   No.

Stan   You bin courtin' three years. Why ent you married yit?

Beatie (*slightly embarrassed*)   We ent sure yit.

Stan   You ent sure you say? What ent you sure of? You know how to do it don't you?

Jenny   Go on wi' you to bed Stan Mann.

Stan   Tell your boy he don't wanna waste too much time or I'll be hevin' yer myself for breakfast – on a plate.

Jenny   Stan Mann, I'm sendin' you to your bed – go on now, off wi' you, you can see Beatie in the mornin'.

Stan (*as he is ushered out – to* **Beatie**)   She's fat ent she? I'm not sayin' she won't do mind, but she's fat. (*As he goes out.*) All right ole sweetheart, I'm goin'. I'm just right for bed. Did you see the new bridge they're building? It's a rum ole thing isn't it . . . (*Out of sound.*)

Jenny *makes up bed on couch for* **Beatie**.

Jimmy   Well, I'm ready for bed.

Beatie   I can't bear sick men. They smell.

Jimmy   Ole Stan's all right – do anythin' for you.

Beatie   I couldn't look after one you know.

Jimmy   Case of hevin' to sometimes.

Beatie   Ronnie's father's paralysed like that. I can't touch him.

Jimmy   Who see to him then?

Beatie   His mother. She wash him, change him, feed him. Ronnie help sometimes. I couldn't though. Ronnie say, 'Christ, woman, I hope you aren't around when I'm ill.' (*Shudders.*) Ole age terrify me.

Jimmy   You sleepin' on that ole couch tonight?

Beatie   Suppose so.

Jimmy   You comfortable sleepin' on that ole thing? You wanna sleep with Jenny while you're here?

Beatie   No thanks, Jimmy. (*She is quite subdued now.*) I'm all right on there.

Jimmy   Right, then I'm off. (*Looking around.*) Where's the *Evening News* I brought in?

Jenny (*entering*)   You off to bed?

Jimmy   Yearp. Reckon I've had 'nough of this ole day. Where's my *News*?

Jenny   Where d'you put it Beatie?

Jimmy (*suddenly seeing the room*)   Blust, you movin' out?

Beatie   Here you are Jimmy Beales. (*Hands him paper.*) It's all tidy now.

Jimmy   So I see. Won't last long though will it? 'Night. (*Goes to bed.*)

Jenny   Well I'm ready for my bed too – how about you Beatie?

Beatie   Yearp.

Jenny (*taking a candle in a stick and lighting it*)   Here, keep this with you. Your bed's made. Want a drink before you turn in?

Beatie   No thanks gal.

Jenny (*picking up Tilley lamp. Leaving*)   Right then. Sleep well gal.

Beatie   Good night Jenny. (*Pause. Loud whispers from now on.*) Hey Jenny.

Jenny   What is it?

Beatie   I'll bake you some pastries when I get to Mother's.

Jenny   Father won't let you use his electricity for me, don't talk daft.

Beatie   I'll get Mother on him. It'll be all right. Your ole ovens weren't big 'nough anyways. Good night.

Moves to door.

Jenny   Good night.

Beatie (*an afterthought*)   Hey Jenny.

Jenny (*returning*)   What now?

Beatie   Did I tell you I took up painting?

Jenny   Painting?

Beatie   Yes – on cardboard and canvases with brushes.

Jenny   What kind of painting?

Beatie   Abstract painting – designs and patterns and such like. I can't do nothing else. I sent two on 'em home. Show you when you come round – if Mother hevn't thrown them out.

Jenny   You're an artist then?

Pause. Such a thought had not occurred to her before. It pleases, even thrills, her.

Beatie   Yes. Good night.

Jenny   Good night.

Beatie *is left alone. Looks out of window. Blows out candle. We see only the faint glow of moonlight from outside and then –*

The curtain falls.

Act Two

Scene One

Two days have passed. **Beatie** *will arrive at her own home, the home of her parents. This is a tied cottage on a main road between two large villages. It is neat and ordinary inside. We can see a large kitchen – where most of the living is done – and attached to it is a large larder; also part of the front room and a piece of the garden where some washing is hanging.*

Mrs Bryant *is a short, stout woman of fifty. She spends most of the day on her own, and consequently when she has a chance to speak to anybody she says as much as she can as fast as she can. The only people she sees are the tradesmen, her husband, the family when they pop in occasionally. She speaks very loudly all the time so that her friendliest tone sounds aggressive, and she manages to dramatise the smallest piece of gossip into something significant. Each piece of gossip is a little act done with little looking at the person to whom it is addressed. At the moment she is at the door leading to the garden, looking for the cat.*

Mrs Bryant   Cossie, Cossie, Cossie, Cossie, Cossie, Cossie! Here Cossie! Food Cossie! Cossie, Cossie, Cossie! Blust you cat, where the hell are you. Oh hell on you then, I ent wastin' my time wi' you now.

She returns to the kitchen and thence the larder, from which she emerges with some potatoes. These she starts peeling. **Stan Mann** *appears round the back door. He has a handkerchief to his nose and is blowing vigorously, as vigorously as his paralysis will allow.* **Mrs Bryant** *looks up, but continues her peeling.*

Stan   Rum thing to git a cold in summer, what you say Daphne?

Mrs Bryant   What'd you have me say my manny. Sit you down bor and rest a bit. Shouldn't wear such daf' clothes.

Stan   Daf' clothes? Blust woman! I got on half a cow's hide, what you sayin'! Where's the gal?

Mrs Bryant   Beatie? She ent come yit. Didn't *you* see her?

Stan   Hell, I was up too early for her. She always stay the weekend wi' Jenny 'fore comin' home?

Mrs Bryant   Most times.

Stan *sneezes.*

Mrs Bryant   What you doin' up this way wi' a cold like that then? Get you home to bed.

Stan   Just come this way to look at the vicarage. Stuff's comin' up for sale soon.

Mrs Bryant   You still visit them things then?

Stan   Yearp. Pass the ole time away. Pass the ole time.

Mrs Bryant   Time drag heavy then?

Stan   Yearp. Time drag heavy. She do that. Time drag so slow, I get to thinkin' it's Monday when it's still Sunday. Still, I had my day gal I say. Yearp. I had that all right.

Mrs Bryant   Yearp. You had that an' a bit more ole son. I shan't grumble if I last as long as you.

Stan   Yearp. I hed my day. An' I'd do it all the same again, you know that? Do it all the same I would.

Mrs Bryant   Blust! All your drinkin' an' that?

Stan   Hell! Thaas what kep' me goin' look. Almost anyways. None o' them young 'uns'll do it, hell if they will. There ent much life in the young 'uns. Bunch o' weak-kneed ruffians. None on 'em like livin' look, none on 'em! You read in them ole papers what go on look, an' you wonder if they can see. You do! Wonder if they got eyes to look around them. Think they know where they live? 'Course they don't, they don't you know, not one. Blust! the winter go an' the spring come on after an' they don't see buds an' they don't smell no breeze an' they don't see gals, an' when they see gals they don't know whatta do wi' 'em. They don't!

Mrs Bryant   Oh hell, they know *that* all right.

Stan   Gimme my young days an' I'd show 'em. Public demonstrations I'd give!

Mrs Bryant   Oh shut you up Stan Mann.

Stan   Just gimme young days again Daphne Bryant an' I'd mount you. (*Pause.*) But they 'ont come again will they gal?

Mrs Bryant   That they 'ont. My ole days working in the fields with them other gals, thems 'ont come again, either.

Stan   No, they 'ont that! Rum ole things the years ent they? (*Pause.*) Them young 'uns is all right though. Long as they don't let no one fool them, long as they think it out theirselves. (*Sneezes and coughs.*)

Mrs Bryant (*moving to help him up*)   Now get you back home Stan Mann. (*Good-naturedly.*) Blust, I aren't hevin' no dead 'uns on me look. Take a rum bor, take a rum an' a drop o' hot milk and get to bed. What's Mrs Mann thinking of lettin' you out like this.

She pulls the coat round the old man and pushes him off. He goes off mumbling and she returns, also mumbling, to her peeling.

Stan   She's a good gal, she's right 'nough, she don't think I got it this bad. I'll pull this ole scarf round me. Hed this scarf a long time, hed it since I started wi' me cars. *She* bought it me. Lasted a long time. Shouldn't need it this weather though . . . (*Exits.*)

Mrs Bryant (*mumbling same time as* **Stan**)   Go on, off you go. Silly ole bugger, runnin' round with a cold like that. Don't know what 'e's doin' half the time. Poor ole man. Cossie? Cossie? That you Cossie? (*Looks through door into front room and out of window at* **Stan**.) Poor ole man.

After peeling for some seconds she turns the radio on, turning the dial knob through all manner of stations and back again until she finds some very loud dance music which she leaves blaring on. Audible to us, but not to **Mrs Bryant**, *is the call of 'Yoo-hoo Mother, yoo-hoo.'* **Beatie** *appears round the garden and peers into the kitchen.* **Mrs Bryant** *jumps.*

Mrs Bryant   Blust, you made me jump.

Beatie (*toning radio down*)   Can't you hear it? Hello, Mother. (*Kisses her.*)

Mrs Bryant   Well, you've arrived then.

Beatie   Didn't you get my card?

Mrs Bryant   Came this morning.

Beatie   Then you knew I'd arrive.

Mrs Bryant   'Course I did.

Beatie   My things come?

Mrs Bryant   One suitcase, one parcel in brown paper –

Beatie   My paintings.

Mrs Bryant   And one other case.

Beatie   My pick-up. D'you see it?

Mrs Bryant   I hevn't touched a thing.

Beatie   Bought myself a pick-up on the HP.

Mrs Bryant   Don't you go telling that to Pearl.

Beatie   Why not?

Mrs Bryant   She'll wanna know why you didn't buy off her on the club.

Beatie   Well, hell, Mother, I weren't gonna hev an ole pick-up sent me from up north somewhere when we lived next door to a gramophone shop.

Mrs Bryant   No. Well, what bus you come on – the half-past-ten one?

Beatie   Yearp. Picked it up on the ole bridge near Jenny's.

Mrs Bryant   Well I looked for you on the half-past-nine bus and you weren't on that so I thought to myself I bet she come on the half-past-ten and you did. You see ole Stan Mann?

Beatie   Was that him just going up the road?

Mrs Bryant   Wearin' an ole brown scarf, that was him.

Beatie   I see him! Just as I were comin' off the bus. Blust! Jimmy Beales give him a real dowsin' down on his allotment 'cos he had an accident.

Mrs Bryant   What, another?

Beatie   Yearp.

Mrs Bryant   Poor ole man. Thaas what give him that cold then. He come in here sneezin' fit to knock hisself down.

Beatie   Poor ole bugger. Got any tea Ma? I'm gonna unpack.

Beatie *goes into front room with case. We see her take out frocks, which she puts on hangers, and underwear and blouses, which she puts on couch.*

Mrs Bryant   Did you see my flowers as you come in? Got some of my hollyhocks still flowering. Creeping up the wall they are – did you catch a glimpse on 'em? And my asters and geraniums? Poor ole Joe Simonds gimme those afore he died. Lovely geraniums they are.

Beatie   Yearp.

Mrs Bryant   When's Ronnie coming?

Beatie   Saturday week – an' Mother, I'm heving all the family along to meet him when he arrive so you patch your rows wi' them.

Mrs Bryant   What you on about gal? What rows wi' them?

Beatie   You know full well what rows I mean – them ones you hev wi' Pearl and Susan.

Mrs Bryant   'Tent so likely. They hev a row wi' me gal but I give 'em no heed, that I don't. (*Hears van pass on road.*) There go Sam Martin's fish van. He'll be calling along here in an hour.

Beatie (*entering with very smart dress*)   Like it Mother?

Mrs Bryant   Blust gal, that's a good 'un ent it! Where d'you buy that then?

Beatie   Swan and Edgar's.

Mrs Bryant   Did Ronnie choose it?

Beatie   Yearp.

Mrs Bryant   He've got good taste then.

Beatie   Yearp. Now listen Mother, I don't want any on you to let me down. When Ronnie come I want him to see we're proper. I'll buy you another bowl so's you don't wash up in the same one as you wash your hands in and I'll get some more tea cloths so's you 'ont use the towels. And no swearin'.

Mrs Bryant   Don't he swear then?

Beatie   He swear all right, only I don't want him to hear *you* swear.

Mrs Bryant   Hev you given it up then?

Beatie   Mother, I've never swore.

Mrs Bryant   Go to hell, listen to her!

Beatie   I never did, now! Mother, I'm *telling* you, listen to me. Ronnie's the best thing I've ever had and I've tried hard for three years to keep hold of him. I don't care what you do when he's gone but don't show me up when he's here.

Mrs Bryant   Speak to your father gal.

Beatie   Father too. I don't want Ronnie to think I come from a small-minded family. 'I can't bear mean people,' he say. 'I don't care about their education, I don't care about their past as long as their minds are large and inquisitive, as long as they're generous.'

Mrs Bryant   Who say that?

Beatie   Ronnie.

Mrs Bryant   He *talk* like that?

Beatie   Yearp.

Mrs Bryant   Sounds like a preacher.

Beatie (*standing on a chair*) 'I don't care if you call me a preacher, I've got something to say and I'm going to say it. I don't care if you don't like being told things – we've come to a time when you've got to say this is right and this is wrong. God in heaven, have we got to be wet all the time? Well, have we?' Christ, Mother, you've got them ole wasps still flying around. (*She waves her arms in the air flaying the wasps.*) September and you've still got wasps. Owee! shoo-shoo! (*In the voice of her childhood.*) Mammy, Mammy, take them ole things away. I doesn't like them – ohh! Nasty things.

Beatie *jumps off chair and picks up a coat-hanger. Now both she and her mother move stealthily around the room 'hunting' wasps. Occasionally* **Mrs Bryant** *strikes one dead or* **Beatie** *spears one against the wall.* **Mrs Bryant** *conducts herself matter-of-fact-like but* **Beatie** *makes a fiendish game of it.*

Mrs Bryant   They're after them apples on that tree outside. Go on! Off wi' you! Outside now! There – that's got 'em out, but I bet the buggers'll be back in a jiffy look.

Beatie   Oh yes, an' I want to have a bath.

Mrs Bryant   When d'you want that then?

Beatie   This morning.

Mrs Bryant   You can't hev no bath this morning, that copper won't heat up till after lunch.

Beatie   Then I'll bake the pastries for Jenny this morning and you can put me water on now. (*She returns to sort her clothes.*)

Mrs Bryant   I'll do that now then. I'll get you the soft water from the tank.

Mrs Bryant *now proceeds to collect bucket and move back and forth between the garden out of view and the copper in the kitchen. She fills the copper with about three buckets of water and then lights the fire underneath. In between buckets she chats.*

(*Off – as she hears lorry go by.*) There go Danny Oakley to market. (*She returns with first bucket.*)

Beatie   Mother! I dreamt I died last night and heaven were at the bottom of a pond. You had to jump in and sink and you know how afeared I am of water. It was full of film stars and soldiers and there were two rooms. In one room they was playing skiffle and – and – I can't remember what were goin' on in the other. Now who was God? I can't remember. It was someone we knew, a she. (*Returns to unpacking.*)

Mrs Bryant (*entering with second bucket; automatically*)   Yearp. (*Pause.*) You hear what happened to the headache doctor's patient? You know what they say about him – if you've got a headache you're all right but if you've got something more you've had it! Well he told a woman not to worry about a lump she complained of under her breast and you know what that were? That turned out to be thrombosis! There! Thrombosis! She had that breast off. Yes, she did. Had to hev it cut off. (*Goes for next bucket.*)

Beatie (*automatically*)   Yearp.

She appears from front room with two framed paintings. She sets them up and admires them. They are primitive designs in bold masses, rather well-balanced shapes and bright poster colours – red, black, and yellow – see Dusty Wesker's work.

Mother! Did I write and tell you I've took up painting? I started five months ago. Working in gouache. Ronnie says I'm good. Says I should carry on and maybe I can sell them for curtain designs. 'Paint girl,' he say. 'Paint! The world is full of people who don't do the things they want so you paint and give us all hope!'

Mrs Bryant *enters.*

Beatie   Like 'em?

Mrs Bryant (*looks at them a second*)   Good colours ent they. (*She is unmoved and continues to empty a third bucket while* **Beatie** *returns paintings to other room.*) Yes gal, I ent got no row wi' Pearl but I ask her to change my Labour Tote man 'cos I wanted to give the commission to Charlie Gorleston and she didn't do it.

Well, if she can be like that I can be like that too. You gonna do some baking you say?

Beatie (*enters from front room putting on a pinafore and carrying a parcel*)   Right now. Here y'are Daphne Bryant, present for you. I want eggs, flour, sugar, and marg. I'm gonna bake a sponge and give it frilling. (*Goes to larder to collect things.*)

Mrs Bryant (*unpacking parcel; it is a pinafore*)   We both got one now.

Mrs Bryant *continues to peel potatoes as* **Beatie** *proceeds to separate four eggs, the yolks of which she starts whipping with sugar. She sings meanwhile a ringing folk song.*

Beatie
Oh a dialogue I'll sing you as true as me life.
Between a coal owner and a poor pitman's wife
As she was a-walking along the highway
She met a coal owner and to him did say
    Derry down, down, down Derry down.

'Whip the eggs till they're light yellow,' he say.

Mrs Bryant   Who say?

Beatie   Ronnie.

Good morning Lord Firedamp the good woman said
I'll do you no harm sir so don't be afraid
If you'd been where I'd been for most of my life
You wouldn't turn pale at a poor pitman's wife
    Singing down, down, down Derry down.

Mrs Bryant   What song's that?

Beatie   A coalmining song.

Mrs Bryant   I tell you what I reckon's a good song, that 'I'll wait for you in the heavens blue'. I reckon that's a lovely song I do. Jimmy Samson he sing that.

Beatie   It's like twenty other songs, it don't mean anything and it's sloshy and sickly.

Mrs Bryant   Yes, I reckon that's a good song that.

Beatie (*suddenly*)   Listen Mother, let me see if I can explain something to you. Ronnie always say that's the point of knowing people. 'It's no good having friends who scratch each other's back,' he say. 'The excitement in knowing people is to hand on what you know and to learn what you don't know. Learn from me,' he say, 'I don't know much but learn what I know.' So let me try and explain to you what he explain to me.

Mrs Bryant (*on hearing a bus*)   There go the half-past-eleven bus to Diss – blust that's early. (*Puts spuds in saucepan on oven and goes to collect runner beans, which she prepares.*)

Beatie   Mother, I'm *talking* to you. Blust woman it's not often we get together and really talk, it's nearly always me listening to you telling who's dead. Just listen a second.

Mrs Bryant   Well go on gal, but you always take so long to say it.

Beatie   What are the words of that song?

Mrs Bryant   I don't know all the words.

Beatie   I'll tell you. (*Recites them.*)

> I'll wait for you in the heavens blue
> As my arms are waiting now.
> Please come to me and I'll be true
> My love shall not turn sour.
> I hunger, I hunger, I cannot wait longer,
> My love shall not turn sour.

There! Now what do that mean?

Mrs Bryant (*surprised*)   Well, don't you know what that mean?

Beatie   I mean what do they do to you? How do the words affect you? Are you moved? Do you find them beautiful?

Mrs Bryant   Them's as good words as any.

Beatie   But do they make you feel better?

Mrs Bryant   Blust gal! That ent meant to be a laxative!

Beatie   I must be mad to talk with you.

Mrs Bryant   Besides it's the tune I like. Words never mean anything.

Beatie   All right, the tune then! What does *that* do to you? Make your belly go gooey, your heart throb, make your head spin with passion? Yes, passion, Mother, know what it is? Because you won't find passion in that third-rate song, no you won't!

Mrs Bryant   Well all right gal, so it's third-rate you say. Can you say why? What make that third-rate and them frilly bits of opera and concert first-rate? 'Sides, did I write that song? Beatie Bryant, you do go up and down in your spirits, and I don't know what's gotten into you gal, no I don't.

Beatie   I don't know either, Mother. I'm worried about Ronnie I suppose. I have that same row with him. I ask him exactly the same questions – what make a pop song third-rate. And he answer and I don't know what he talk about. Something about registers, something about commercial world blunting our responses. 'Give yourself time woman,' he say. 'Time! You can't learn how to live overnight. *I* don't even know,' he say, 'and half the world don't know but we got to try. Try,' he says, ''cos we're still suffering from the shock of two world wars and we don't know it. Talk,' he say, 'and look and listen and think and ask questions.' But Jesus! I don't know what questions to ask or *how* to talk. And he gets so riled – and yet sometimes so nice. 'It's all going up in flames,' he say, 'but I'm going to make bloody sure I save someone from the fire.'

Mrs Bryant   Well I'm sure *I* don't know what he's on about. Turn to your baking gal look and get you done, Father'll be home for his lunch in an hour.

A faint sound of an ambulance is heard. **Mrs Bryant** *looks up but says nothing.* **Beatie** *turns to whipping the eggs again and* **Mrs Bryant** *to cleaning up the runner beans. Out of this pause* **Mrs Bryant** *begins* *to sing 'I'll wait for you in the heavens blue', but on the second line she hums the tune incorrectly.*

Beatie (*laughs*)   No, no, hell Mother, it don't go like that. It's –

Beatie *corrects her and in helping her mother she ends by singing the song, with some enthusiasm, to the end.*

Mrs Bryant   Thank God you come home sometimes gal – you do bring a little life with you anyway.

Beatie   Mother, I ent never heard you express a feeling like that.

Mrs Bryant (*she is embarrassed*)   The world don't want no feelings gal. (*Footsteps are heard.*) Is that your father home already?

Mr Bryant *appears at the back door and lays a bicycle against the wall. He is a small shrivelled man wearing denims, a peaked cap, boots, and gaiters. He appears to be in some pain.*

Beatie   Hello poppy Bryant.

Mr Bryant   Hello Beatie. You're here then.

Mrs Bryant   What are you home so early for?

Mr Bryant   The ole guts ache again. (*Sits in armchair and grimaces.*)

Mrs Bryant   Well, what is it?

Mr Bryant   Blust woman, I don't know what 'tis n'more'n you, do I?

Mrs Bryant   Go to the doctor man I keep telling you.

Beatie   What is it father Bryant?

Mrs Bryant   He got guts ache.

Beatie   But what's it from?

Mr Bryant   I've just said I don't know.

Mrs Bryant   Get you to a doctor man, don't be so soft. You don't want to be kept from work do you?

Mr Bryant   That I don't, no I don't. Hell, I just see ole Stan Mann picked up an' thaas upset me enough.

Mrs Bryant   Picked up you say?

Mr Bryant   Well, didn't you hear the ambulance?

Mrs Bryant   There! I hear it but I didn't say narthin'. Was that for Stan Mann then?

Mr Bryant   I was cycling along wi' Jack Stones and we see this here figure on the side o' the road there an' I say, thaas a rum shape in the road Jack, and he say, blust, that's ole Stan Mann from Heybrid, an' 'twere. 'Course soon ever he see what 'twere, he rushed off for 'n ambulance and I waited alongside Stan.

Beatie   But he just left here.

Mrs Bryant   I see it comin'. He come in here an' I shoved him off home. Get you to bed and take some rum an' a drop o' hot milk, I tell him.

Beatie   Is he gonna die?

Mr Bryant   Wouldn't surprise me that it wouldn't. Blust, he look done in.

Mrs Bryant   Poor ole fellah. Shame though ent it?

Mr Bryant   When d'you arrive Beatie?

Mrs Bryant   She come on the half-past-ten bus. I looked for her on the nine-thirty bus and she weren't on that, so I thought to myself I bet she come on the half-past-ten. She did.

Mr Bryant   Yearp.

Mrs Bryant   You gonna stay away all day?

Mr Bryant   No I aren't. I gotta go back 'cos one of the ole sows is piggin'. 'Spect she'll be hevin' them in a couple of hours. (*To* **Beatie**.) Got a sow had a litter o' twenty-two. (*Picks up paper to read.*)

Beatie   Twenty-two? Oh Pop, can I come see this afternoon?

Mr Bryant   Yearp.

Mrs Bryant   Thought you was hevin' a bath.

Beatie   Oh yes, I forgot. I'll come tomorrow then.

Mr Bryant   They'll be there. What you doin' gal?

Mrs Bryant   She's baking a sponge, now leave her be.

Mr Bryant   Oh, you learnt something in London then.

Beatie   Ronnie taught me.

Mr Bryant   Well where *is* Ronnie then?

Mrs Bryant   He's comin' on Saturday a week an' the family's goin' to be here to greet him.

Mr Bryant   All on 'em?

Mrs Bryant *and* **Beatie**   All on 'em!

Mr Bryant   Well that'll be a rum gatherin' then.

Mrs Bryant   And we've to be on our best behaviour.

Mr Bryant   No cussin' and swearin'?

Mrs Bryant *and* **Beatie**   No.

Mr Bryant   Blust, I shan't talk then.

A young man, **Mr Healey**, *appears round the garden – he is the farmer's son, and manager of the estate* **Bryant** *works for.*

Mrs Bryant (*seeing him first*)   Oh, Mr Healey, yes. Jack! It's Mr Healey.

Mr Bryant *rises and goes to the door.* **Healey** *speaks in a firm, not unkind, but business-is-business voice. There is that apologetic threat even in his politeness.*

Mr Healey   You were taken ill.

Mr Bryant   It's all right, sir, only guts ache, won't be long goin'. The pigs is all seen to, just waiting for the ole sow to start.

Mr Healey   What time you expecting it?

Mr Bryant   Oh, she 'ont come afore two this afternoon, no she 'ont be much afore that.

Mr Healey   You're sure you're well, Jack? I've been thinking that it's too much for you carting those pails round the yard.

Mr Bryant   No, that ent too heavy, sir, 'course 'tent. You don't wanna worry, I'll be along after lunch. Just an ole guts ache that's all – seein' the doctor tonight – eat too fast probably.

Mr Healey   If you're sure you're all right, then I'll put young Daniels off. You can manage without him now we've fixed the new pump in.

Mr Bryant   I can manage, sir – 'course I can.

Mr Healey (*moving off outside*)   All right then, Jack, I'll be with you around two o'clock. I want to take the old one out of number three and stick her with the others in seventeen. The little ones won't need her, will they? Then we'll have them sorted out tomorrow.

Mr Bryant   That's right, sir, they *can* go on their own now, they can. I'll see to it tomorrow.

Mr Healey   Right then, Jack. Oh – you hear Stan Mann died?

Mr Bryant   He died already? But I saw him off in the ambulance no more'n half-hour ago.

Mr Healey   Died on the way to hospital. Jack Stones told me. Lived in Heybrid, didn't he?

Mr Bryant   Alongside my daughter.

Mr Healey (*calling*)   Well, good morning, Mrs Bryant.

Mrs Bryant (*calling*)   Good morning, Mr Healey.

The two men nod to each other, **Mr Healey** *goes off.* **Mr Bryant** *lingers a second.*

Mrs Bryant (*to* **Beatie**)   That was Mr Healey, the new young manager.

Beatie   I know it Mother.

Mr Bryant (*returning slowly*)   He's dead then.

Mrs Bryant   Who? Not Stan Mann!

Mr Bryant   Young Healey just tell me.

Mrs Bryant   Well I go t'hell. An' he were just here look, just here alongside o' me not more'n hour past.

Mr Bryant   Rum ent it?

Beatie (*weakly*)   Oh hell, I hate dying.

Mrs Bryant   He were a good ole bor though. Yes he was. A good ole stick. There!

Beatie   Used to ride me round on his horse, always full o' life an' jokes. 'Tell your boy he wanna hurry up and marry you,' he say to me, 'or I'll hev you meself on a plate.'

Mrs Bryant   He were a one for smut though.

Beatie   I was talkin' with him last night. Only last night he was tellin' me how he caught me pinchin' some gooseberries off his patch an' how he gimme a whole apron full and I went into one o' his fields near by an' ate the lot. 'Blust,' he say, 'you had the ole guts ache,' an' he laugh, sat there laughin' away to hisself.

Mrs Bryant   I can remember that. Hell, Jenny'll miss him – used always to pop in an' out o' theirs.

Beatie   Seem like the whole world gone suddenly dead don' it?

Mr Bryant   Rum ent it?

Silence.

Mrs Bryant   *He's* a nice man Mr Healey is, yes he is, a good sort, I like him.

Beatie   Don't know about being nice. Sounds to me like he were threatening to sack Father.

Mr Bryant   That's what I say see, get a rise and they start cutting down the men or the overtime.

Mrs Bryant   The Union magazine's come.

Mr Bryant   I don't want that ole thing.

Beatie   Why can't you do something to stop the sackings?

Mr Bryant   You can't, you can't – that's what I say, you can't. Sharp as a pig's scream they are – you just *can't* do nothin'.

Beatie   Mother, where's the bakin' tin?

Mr Bryant   When we gonna eat that?

Beatie   You ent! It's for Jenny Beales.

Mr Bryant   You aren't making that for Jenny are you?

Beatie   I promised her.

Mr Bryant   Not with my electricity you aren't.

Beatie   But I promised, Poppy.

Mr Bryant   That's no matters. I aren't spendin' money on electricity bills so's you can make every Tom, Dick 'n' Harry a sponge cake, that I aren't.

Mrs Bryant   Well, don't be so soft man, it won't take more'n half-hour's bakin'.

Mr Bryant   I don't care what it'll take I say. I aren't lettin' her. Jenny wants cakes, she can make 'em herself. So put that away Beatie and use it for something else.

Mrs Bryant   You wanna watch what you're sayin' of 'cos I live here too.

Mr Bryant   I know all about that but I pay the electricity bill and I says she isn't bakin'.

Beatie   But Poppy, one cake.

Mr Bryant   No I say.

Beatie   Well, Mummy, do something – how can he be so mean.

Mrs Bryant   Blust me if you ent the meanest ole sod that walks this earth. Your own daughter and you won't let her use your oven. You bloody ole hypercrite.

Mr Bryant   You pay the bills and then you call names.

Mrs Bryant   What I ever seen in you God only knows. Yes! an' he never warn me. Bloody ole hypercrite!

Mr Bryant   You pay the bills and then you call names I say.

Mrs Bryant   On four pounds ten a week? You want me to keep you *and* pay bills? Four pound ten he give me. God knows what he do wi' the rest. I don't know how much he've got. I don't, no I don't. Bloody ole hypercrite.

Mr Bryant   Let's hev grub and not so much o' the lip woman.

Beatie *begins to put the things away. She is on the verge of the tears she will soon let fall.*

Mrs Bryant   That's how he talk to me – when he do talk. 'Cos you know he don't ever talk more'n he hev to, and when he do say something it's either 'how much this cost' or 'lend us couple o' bob'. He've got the money but sooner than break into that he borrow off me. Bloody old miser. (*To* **Beatie**.) What you wanna cry for gal? 'Tent worth it. Blust, you don't wanna let an ole hypercrite like him upset you, no you don't. I'll get my back on you my manny, see if I don't. You won't get away with no tricks on me.

Beatie *has gone into the other room and returned with a small packet.*

Beatie (*throwing parcel in father's lap*)   Present for you.

Mrs Bryant   I'd give him presents that I would! I'd walk out and disown him! Beatie, now stop you a-cryin' gal – blust, he ent worth cryin' for, that he ent. Stop it I say and we'll have lunch. Or you lost your appetite gal?

Beatie *sniffs a few tears back, pauses, and –*

Beatie   No – no, that I ent. Hell, I can eat all right!

Curtain.

Scene Two

Lunch has been eaten. **Mr Bryant** *is sitting at the table rolling himself a cigarette.* **Mrs Bryant** *is collecting the dishes and taking them to a sink to wash up.* **Beatie** *is taking things off the table and putting them into the larder – jars of sauce, plates of sliced bread and cakes, butter, sugar, condiments, and bowl of tinned fruit.*

Mrs Bryant (*to* **Beatie**)   Ask him what he want for his tea.

Mr Bryant   She don't ever ask me before, what she wanna ask me now for?

Mrs Bryant   Tell him it's his stomach I'm thinking about – I don't want him complaining to me about the food I cook.

Mr Bryant   Tell her it's no matters to me – I ent got no pain now besides.

Beatie   Mother, is that water ready for my bath?

Mrs Bryant   Where you hevin' it?

Beatie   In the kitchen of course.

Mrs Bryant   Blust gal, you can't bath in this kitchen during the day, what if someone call at the door?

Beatie   Put up the curtain then, I shan't be no more'n ten minutes.

Mr Bryant   'Sides, who wants to see her in her dickey suit.

Beatie   I know men as 'ould pay to see me in my dickey suit. (*Posing her plump outline.*) Don't you think I got a nice dickey suit?

Mr Bryant *makes a dive and pinches her bottom.*

Beatie   Ow! Stoppit Bryants, stoppit!

He persists.

Daddy, stop it now!

Mrs Bryant   Tell him he can go as soon as he like, I want your bath over and done with.

Beatie   Oh Mother, stop this nonsense do. If you want to tell him something tell him – not me.

Mrs Bryant   *I* don't want to speak to him, hell if I do.

Beatie   Father, get the bath in for me please. Mother, where's them curtains.

Mr Bryant *goes off to fetch a long tin bath – wide at one end, narrow at the other – while* **Mrs Bryant** *leaves washing-up to fish out some curtains which she hangs from one wall to another concealing thus a corner of the kitchen. Anything that is in the way is removed.* **Beatie** *meanwhile brings out a change of underwear, her dressing-gown, the new frock, some soap, powder, and towel. These she lays within easy reach of the curtain.*

Beatie   I'm gonna wear my new dress and go across the fields to see Frankie and Pearl.

Mrs Bryant   Frankie won't be there, what you on about? He'll be gettin' the harvest in.

Beatie   You makin' anything for the harvest festival?

Mr Bryant (*entering with bath, places it behind curtain*)   Your mother don't ever do anything for the harvest festival – don't you know that by now.

Beatie   Get you to work father Bryant, I'm gonna plunge in water and I'll make a splash.

Mrs Bryant   Tell him we've got kippers for tea and if he don' want none let him say now.

Beatie   She says it's kippers for tea.

Mr Bryant   Tell her I'll eat kippers. (*Goes off, collecting bike on the way.*)

Beatie   He says he'll eat kippers. Right now, Mother, you get cold water an' I'll pour the hot.

Each now picks up a bucket. **Mrs Bryant** *goes off out to collect the cold water and* **Beatie** *plunges bucket into boiler to retrieve hot water. The bath is prepared with much childlike glee.* **Beatie** *loves her creature comforts and does with unabashed, almost animal, enthusiasm that which she enjoys. When the bath is prepared,* **Beatie** *slips behind the curtain to undress and enter.*

Mrs Bryant   You hear about Jimmy Skelton? They say he've bin arrested for accosting some man in the village.

Beatie   Jimmy Skelton what own the pub?

Mrs Bryant   That's him. I know all about Jimmy Skelton though. He were a young boy when I were a young girl. I always partner him at whist drives. He's been to law before you know. Yes! An' he won the day too! Won the day he did. I don't take notice though, him and me gets on all right. What do Ronnie's mother do with her time?

Beatie   She've got a sick husband to look after.

Mrs Bryant   She an educated woman?

Beatie   Educated? No. She's a foreigner. Nor ent Ronnie educated neither. He's an intellectual, failed all his exams. They read and things.

Mrs Bryant   Oh, they don't do nothing then?

Beatie   Do nothing? I'll tell you what Ronnie do, he work till all hours in a hot ole kitchen. An' he teach kids in a club to act and jive and such. And he don't stop at weekends either 'cos then there's political meetings and such and I get breathless trying to keep up wi' him. Oooh, Mother it's hot . . .

Mrs Bryant   I'll get you some cold then.

Beatie   No – ooh – it's lovely. The water's so soft Mother.

Mrs Bryant   Yearp.

Beatie   It's so soft and smooth. I'm in.

Mrs Bryant   Don't you stay in too long gal. There go the twenty-minutes-past-one bus.

Beatie   Oh Mother, me bath cubes. I forgot me bath cubes. In the little case by me pick-up.

Mrs Bryant *finds bath cubes and hands them to* **Beatie**.

Mrs Bryant (*continuing her work*)   I shall never forget when I furse heard on it. I was in the village and I was talking to Reggie Fowler. I say to him, there've bin a lot o' talk about Jimmy ent there? Disgustin', I say. Still, there's somebody wanna make some easy money, you'd expect that in a village wouldn't you? Yes, I say to him, a lot of talk. An' he stood there, an' he were a-lookin' at me an' a-lookin' as I were a-talkin' and then he say, missus, he say, I were one o' the victims! Well, you could've hit me over the head wi' a hammer. I was one o' the victims, he say.

Beatie   Mother, these bath cubes smell beautiful. I could stay here all day.

Mrs Bryant   Still, Jimmy's a good fellow with it all – do anything for you. I partner him at whist drives; he bin had up scores o' times though.

Beatie   Mother, what we gonna make Ronnie when he come?

Mrs Bryant   Well, what do he like?

Beatie   He like trifle and he like steak and kidney pie.

Mrs Bryant   We'll make that then. So long as he don't complain o' the guts ache. Frankie hev it too you know.

Beatie   Know why? You all eat too much. The Londoners think we live a healthy life but they don't know we stuff ourselves silly till our guts ache.

Mrs Bryant   But you know what's wrong wi' Jimmy Beales? It's indigestion. He eat too fast.

Beatie   What the hell's indigestion doin' a'tween his shoulder-blades?

Mrs Bryant   'Cos some people get it so bad it go right through their stomach to the back.

Beatie   You don't get indigestion in the back, Mother, what you on about?

Mrs Bryant   Don't you tell me gal, I hed it!

Beatie   Owee! The soap's in me eyes – Mother, towel, the towel, quickly the towel!

Mrs Bryant *hands in towel to* **Beatie**. *The washing-up is probably done by now, so* **Mrs Bryant** *sits in a chair, legs apart and arms folded, thinking what else to say.*

Mrs Bryant   You heard that Ma Buckley hev been taken to mental hospital in Norwich? Poor ole dear. If there's one thing I can't abide that's mental cases. They frighten me – they do. Can't face 'em. I'd sooner follow a man to a churchyard than the mental hospital. That's a terrible thing to see a person lose their reason – that 'tis. Well, I tell you what, down where I used to live, down the other side of the Hall, years ago we moved in next to an old woman. I only had Jenny and Frank then – an' this woman she were the sweetest of people. We used to talk and do errands for each other – Oh she was a sweet ole dear. And then one afternoon I was going out to get my washin' in and I saw her. She was standin' in a tub o' water up to her neck. She was! Up to her neck. An' her eyes had that glazed, wonderin' look and she stared straight at me she did. Straight at me. Well, do you know what? I was struck *dumb*. I was *struck* dumb wi' shock. What wi' her bein' so nice all this while, the sudden comin' on her like that in the tub fair upset me. It did! And people tell me afterwards that she's bin goin' in an' out o' hospital for years. Blust, that scare me. That scare me so much she nearly took me round the bend wi' her.

Beatie *appears from behind the curtain in her dressing-gown, a towel round her head.*

Beatie   There! I'm gonna hev a bath every day when I'm married.

Beatie *starts rubbing her hair with towel and fiddles with radio. She finds a programme playing Mendelssohn's Fourth Symphony, the slow movement, and stands before the mirror, listening and rubbing.*

(*Looking at her reflection.*) Isn't your nose a funny thing, and your ears. And your arms and your legs, aren't they funny things – sticking out of a lump.

Mrs Bryant (*switching off radio*)   Turn that squit off!

Beatie (*turning on her mother violently*)   *Mother!* I could kill you when you do that. No wonder I don't know anything about anything. I never heard nothing but dance music because you always turned off the classics. I never knowed anything about the news because you always switched off after the headlines. I never read any good books 'cos there was never any in the house.

Mrs Bryant   What's gotten into you now gal?

Beatie   God in heaven Mother, you live in the country but you got no – no – no majesty. You spend your time among green fields, you grow flowers and you breathe fresh air and you got no majesty. Your mind's cluttered up with nothing and you shut out the world. What kind of a life did you give me?

Mrs Bryant   Blust gal, I weren't no teacher.

Beatie   But you hindered. You didn't open one door for me. Even his mother cared more for me than what you did. Beatie, she say, Beatie, why don't you take up evening classes and learn something other than waitressing. Yes, she say, you won't ever regret learnin' things. But did you care what job I took up or whether I learned things? You didn't even think it was necessary.

Mrs Bryant   I fed you. I clothed you. I took you out to the sea. What more d'you want. We're only country folk you know. We ent got no big things here you know.

Beatie   Squit! Squit! It makes no difference country or town. *All* the town girls I ever worked with were just like me. It makes no difference country or town – that's squit. Do you know when I used to work at the holiday camp and I sat down with the other girls to write a letter we used to sit and discuss what we wrote about. An' we all agreed, all on us, that we started: 'Just a few lines to let you know', and then we get on to the weather and then we get stuck so we write about each other and after a page an' half of big scrawl end up: 'Hoping this finds you as well as it leaves me.' There! We couldn't say any more. Thousands of things happening at this holiday camp and we couldn't find words for them. All of us the same. Hundreds of girls and one day we're gonna be mothers, and you *still* talk to me of Jimmy Skelton and the ole woman in the tub. Do you know I've heard that story a dozen times. A dozen times. Can't you hear yourself Mother? Jesus, how can I bring Ronnie to this house.

Mrs Bryant   Blust gal, if Ronnie don't like us then he –

Beatie   Oh, he'll like you all right. He like people. He'd've loved ole Stan Mann. Ole Stan Mann would've understood everything Ronnie talk about. Blust! That man liked livin'. Besides, Ronnie say it's too late for the old 'uns to learn. But he says it's up to us young 'uns. And them of us that know hev got to teach them of us as don't know.

Mrs Bryant I bet he hev a hard time trying to change you gal!

Beatie He's *not* trying to change me Mother. You can't change people, he say, you can only give them some love and hope they'll take it. And he's tryin' to teach me and I'm tryin' to understand – do you see that Mother?

Mrs Bryant I don't see what that's got to do with music though.

Beatie Oh my God! (*Suddenly.*) I'll show you. (*Goes off to front room to collect pick-up and a record.*) Now sit you down gal and I'll show you. Don't start ironing or reading or nothing, just sit there and be prepared to learn something. (*Appears with pick-up and switches on.*) You aren't too old, just you sit and listen. That's the trouble you see, we ent ever prepared to learn anything, we close our minds the minute anything unfamiliar appear. *I* could never listen to music. I used to like some on it but then I'd lose patience, I'd go to bed in the middle of a symphony, or my mind would wander 'cos the music didn't mean anything to me so I'd go to bed or start talking. 'Sit back woman,' he'd say, 'listen to it. Let it happen to you and you'll grow as big as the music itself.'

Mrs Bryant Blust he talk like a book.

Beatie An' sometimes he talk as though you didn't know where the moon or the stars was.

Beatie *puts on record of Bizet's L'Arlésienne Suite.*

Now listen. This is a simple piece of music, it's not highbrow, but it's full of living. And that's what he say socialism is. 'Christ,' he say. 'Socialism isn't talking all the time, it's living, it's singing, it's dancing, it's being interested in what go on around you, it's being concerned about people and the world.' Listen Mother. (*She becomes breathless and excited.*) Listen to it. It's simple isn't it? Can you call that squit?

Mrs Bryant I don't say it's all squit.

Beatie   You don't have to frown because it's alive.

Mrs Bryant   No, not all on it's squit.

Beatie   See the way the other tune comes in? Hear it? Two simple tunes, one after the other.

Mrs Bryant   I aren't saying it's all squit.

Beatie   And now listen, listen, it goes together, the two tunes together, they knit, they're perfect. Don't it make you want to dance? (*She begins to dance a mixture of a cossack dance and a sailor's hornpipe.*)

The music becomes fast and her spirits are young and high.

Listen to that Mother. Is it difficult? Is it squit? It's light. It make me feel light and confident and happy. God, Mother, we could all be so much more happy and alive. Wheeeee . . .

Beatie *claps her hands and dances on and her mother smiles and claps her hands and –*

The curtain falls.

Act Three

Two weeks have passed. It is Saturday, the day Ronnie is to arrive. One of the walls of the kitchen is now pushed aside and the front room is revealed. It is low-ceilinged, and has dark-brown wooden beams. The furniture is not typical country-farmhouse type. There may be one or two Windsor-type straight-back chairs, but for the rest it is cheap utility stuff. Two armchairs, a table, a small bamboo table, wooden chairs, a small sofa, and a swivel bookcase. There are a lot of flowers around – in pots on the window ledge and in vases on the bamboo table and swivel case.

It is three in the afternoon, the weather is cloudy – it has been raining and is likely to start again. On the table is a spread of food (none of this will be eaten). There are cakes and biscuits on plates and glass stands. Bread and butter, butter in a dish, tomatoes, cheese, jars of pickled onions, sausage rolls, dishes of tinned fruit – it is a spread! Round the table are eight chairs. **Beatie***'s paintings are hanging on the wall. The room is empty because* **Beatie** *is upstairs changing and* **Mrs Bryant** *is in the kitchen.* **Beatie** *– until she descends – conducts all her conversation from upstairs.*

Beatie Mother! What you on at now?

Mrs Bryant (*from kitchen*) I'm just puttin' these glass cherries on the trifle.

Beatie Well come on look, he'll be here at four thirty.

Mrs Bryant (*from kitchen*) Don't you fret gal, it's another hour 'n' half yet, the postman hevn't gone by. (*Enters with an enormous bowl of trifle.*) There! He like trifle you say?

Beatie He love it.

Mrs Bryant Well he need to 'cos there's plenty on it. (*To herself, surveying the table.*) Yes, there is, there's plenty on it. (*It starts to rain.*) Blust, listen to that weather.

Beatie Rainin' again!

Mrs Bryant (*looking out of window*)   Raining? It's rainin' fit to drowned you. (*Sound of bus.*) There go the three-o'clock.

Beatie   Mother get you changed, come on, I want us ready in time.

Mrs Bryant   Blust you'd think it were the bloody Prince of Egypt comin'. (*Goes upstairs.*)

The stage is empty again for a few seconds. People are heard taking off their macs and exclaiming at the weather from the kitchen. Enter **Frank** *and* **Pearl Bryant***. He is pleasant and dressed in a blue pin-striped suit, is ruddy-faced and blond-haired. An odd sort of shyness makes him treat everything as a joke. His wife is a pretty brunette, young, and ordinarily dressed in plain, flowered frock.*

Frank (*calling*)   Well, where are you all? Come on – I'm hungry.

Pearl   Shut you up bor, you only just had lunch.

Frank   Well I'm hungry again. (*Calling.*) Well, where is this article we come to see?

Beatie   He ent arrived.

Frank   Well, he want to hurry, 'cos I'm hungry.

Beatie   You're always hungry.

Frank   What do you say he is – a strong socialist?

Beatie   Yes.

Frank   And a Jew boy?

Beatie   Yes.

Frank (*to himself*)   Well, that's a queer mixture then.

Pearl (*calling*)   I hope he don't talk politics all the time.

Frank   Have you had a letter from him yet?

Pearl   Stop it Frank, you know she hevn't heard.

Frank Well that's a rum boy friend what don't write. (*Looks at paintings, pauses before one of them and growls.*)

Pearl Watch out or it'll bite you back.

Beatie *comes down from upstairs. She is dressed in her new frock and looks happy, healthy, and radiant.*

Frank Hail there, sister! I was then contemplating your masterpiece.

Beatie Well don't contemplate too long 'cos you aren't hevin' it.

Frank Blust! I'd set my ole heart on it.

Pearl That's a nice frock Beatie.

Frank Where's the rest of our mighty clan?

Beatie Jenny and Jimmy should be here soon and Susie and Stan mightn't come.

Frank What's wrong wi' them?

Beatie Don't talk to me about it 'cos I hed enough! Susie won't talk to Mother.

Pearl That make nearly eighteen months she hevn't spoke.

Beatie Why ever did *you* and Mother fall out Pearl?

Frank 'Cos Mother's so bloody stubborn that's why.

Pearl Because one day she said she wanted to change her Labour Tote man, that's why, and she asked me to do it for her. So I said all right, but it'll take a couple of weeks; and then she get riled because she said I didn't want to change it for her. And then I ask her why didn't she change him herself and she say because she was too ill to go all the way to see John Clayton to tell him, and then she say to me, why, don't you think I'm ill? And I say – I know this were tactless o' me – but I say, no Mother, you don't look ill to me. And she didn't speak to me since. I only hope she don't snub me this afternoon.

Beatie   Well, she tell me a different story.

Frank   Mother's always quarrelling.

Pearl   Well I reckon there ent much else she *can* do stuck in this ole house on her own all day. And father Bryant he don't say too much when he's home you know.

Frank   Well blust, she hevn't spoke to her own mother for three years, not since Granny Dykes took Jenny in when she had that illegitimate gal Daphne.

Beatie   Hell! What a bloody family!

Frank   A mighty clan I say.

Jimmy *and* **Jenny Beales** *now enter.*

Jenny   Hello Frankie, hello Pearl, hello Beatie.

Frank   And more of the mighty clan.

Jenny   Mighty clan you say? Mighty bloody daft you mean. Well, where is he?

Frank   The mysterious stranger has not yet come – we await.

Jenny   Well, I aren't waitin' long 'cos I'm hungry.

Pearl   That's all this family of Bryants ever do is think o' their guts.

Frank (*to* **Jimmy**)   Have you formed your association yit?

Jenny   What association is this?

Frank   What! Hevn't he told you?

Jimmy   Shut you up Frank Bryant or you'll get me hung.

Frank   Oh, a mighty association – a mighty one! I'll tell ye. One day you see we was all sittin' round in the pub – Jimmy, me, Starkie, Johnny Oats, and Bonky Dawson – we'd hed a few drinks and Jimmy was feelin' – well, he was feelin' – you know what, the itch! He hed the itch! He started complaining about ham, ham, ham all the time. So then Bonky Dawson say, blust, he say, there must be women about who feel the same. And Starkie he say, well 'course they are, only how do you tell? And then we was all quiet a while thinkin' on it when suddenly Jimmy says, we ought to start an association of them as need a bit now and then and we all ought to wear a badge he say, and when you see a woman wearin' a badge you know she need a bit too.

Jimmy   Now that's enough Frank or I'll hit you over the skull.

Frank   Now, not content wi' just that, ole Jimmy then say, and we ought to have a password to indicate how bad off you are. So listen what he suggest. He suggest you go up to any one o' these women what's wearin' a badge and you say, how many lumps of sugar do you take in your tea? And if she say 'two' then you know she ent too badly off, but she's willin'. But if she say 'four' then you know she's in a bad a state as what you are, see?

Long pause.

Jenny   He'd hev a fit if she said she took sixteen lumps though wouldn't he?

Pause.

Pearl   Where's mother Bryant?

Beatie   Uptairs changin'.

Pearl   Where's father Bryant?

Beatie   Tendin' the pigs.

Frank   You're lucky to hev my presence you know.

Beatie   Oh?

Frank   A little more sun and I'd've bin gettin' in the harvest.

Pearl   Well, what did you think of that storm last night? All that thunder 'n' lightnin' and it didn't stop once.

Beatie   Ronnie love it you know. He sit and watch it for bloody hours.

Frank   He's a queer article then.

Jenny   He do sound a rum 'un don't he?

Beatie   Well you'll soon see.

Jimmy   Hev he got any sisters?

Beatie   One married and she live not far from here.

Pearl   She live in the country? A town girl? Whatever for?

Beatie   Her husband make furniture by hand.

Pearl   Can't he do that in London?

Beatie   Ronnie say they think London's an inhuman place.

Jimmy   So 'tis, so 'tis.

Beatie   Here come father Bryant.

Mr Bryant *enters. He is in denims and raincoat, tired, and stooped slightly.*

Frank   And this be the male head of the mighty Bryant clan!

Mr Bryant   Blust, you're all here soon then.

Beatie   Get you changed quick Father – he'll be along any minute look.

Mr Bryant   Shut you up gal, I'll go when I'm ready, I don't want you pushin' me.

Mrs Bryant *comes from upstairs. She looks neat and also wears a flowered frock.*

Frank   And this be the female head o' the mighty Bryant clan!

Mrs Bryant   Come on Bryant, get you changed – we're all ready look.

Mr Bryant   Blust, there go the other one. Who is he this boy, that's what I wanna know.

Mrs Bryant   He's upset! I can see it! I can tell it in his voice. Come on Bryants, what's the matters.

Mr Bryant   There ent much up wi' me, what you on about woman. (*Makes to go.*) Now leave me be, you want me changed look.

Mrs Bryant   If there ent much up wi' you, I'll marry some other.

Frank   Healey bin at you Pop?

Beatie   The pigs dyin'?

Mrs Bryant   It's something serious or he wouldn't be so happy lookin'.

Mr Bryant   I bin put on casual labour.

Jenny   Well isn't that a sod now.

Mrs Bryant   Your guts I suppose.

Mr Bryant   I tell him it's no odds, that there's no pain. That don't matters Jack, he says, I aren't hevin' you break up completely on me. You go on casual, he say, and if you gets better you can come on to the pigs again.

Mrs Bryant   That's half pay then?

Beatie   Can't you get another job?

Frank   He've bin wi' them for eighteen years.

Beatie   But you must be able to do something else – what about cowman again?

Mr Bryant   Bill Waddington do that see. He've bin at it this last six 'n' half years.

Jenny   It's no good upsettin' yourself Beatie. It happen all the time gal.

Jimmy   Well, we told her when she was at ours didn't we.

Mrs Bryant (*to* **Mr Bryant**)   All right, get you on up, there ent nothin' we can do. We'll worry on it later. We always manage. It's gettin' late look.

Mr Bryant   Can he swim? 'Cos he bloody need to. It's rainin' fit to drowned you. (*Goes off upstairs.*)

Mrs Bryant   Well, shall we have a little cup o' tea while we're waitin'? I'll go put the kettle on. (*Goes to kitchen.*)

Everyone sits around now. **Jenny** *takes out some knitting and* **Jimmy** *picks up a paper to read. There is a silence. It is not an awkward silence, just a conversationless room.*

Pearl (*to* **Jenny**)   Who's lookin' after your Daphne?

Jenny   Ole mother Mann next door.

Pearl   Poor ole dear. How's she feelin' now?

Jenny   She took it bad. (*Nodding at* **Jimmy**.) Him too. He think he were to blame.

Pearl   Blust that weren't his fault. Don't be so daft Jimmy Beales. Don't you go fretting yourself or you'll make us all feel queer look. You done nothin' wrong bor – he weren't far off dying 'sides.

Frank   They weren't even married were they?

Jenny   No, they never were – she started lookin' after him when he had that first stroke and she just stayed.

Jimmy   Lost her job 'cos of it too.

Frank   Well, yes, she would, wouldn't she – she was a State Registered Nurse or something weren't she? (*To* **Beatie**.) Soon ever the authorities got to hear o' that they told her to pack up livin' wi' him or quit her job, see?

Jenny   Bloody daft I reckon. What difference it make whether she married him or not.

Pearl   I reckon you miss him Jenny?

Jenny   Hell yes – that I do. He were a good ole bor – always joking and buying the gal sweets. Well, do you know I cry when I heard it? I did. Blust, that fair shook me – that it did, there!

Jimmy   Who's lookin' after *your* kid then, Pearl?

Pearl   Father.

Pause.

Jimmy (*to* **Frank**)   Who do you think'll win today?

Frank   Well Norwich won't.

Jimmy   No.

Pause. **Mrs Bryant** *enters and sits down.*

Mrs Bryant   Well the kettle's on.

Pearl (*to* **Beatie**)   Hev his sister got any children?

Beatie   Two boys.

Jimmy   She wanna get on top one night then they'll hev girls.

Jenny   Oh shut you up Jimmy Beales.

Mrs Bryant   Hed another little win last night.

Jenny   When was this?

Mrs Bryant   The fireman's whist drive. Won seven 'n' six in the knockout.

Jenny   Yearp.

Frank (*reading the paper*)   I see that boy what assaulted the ole woman in London got six years.

Mrs Bryant   Blust! He need to! I'd've given him six years and a bit more. Bloody ole hooligans. Do you give me a chance to pass sentence and I'd soon clear the streets of crime, that I would. Yes, that I would.

Beatie (*springing into activity*)   All right Mother – we'll give you a chance. (*Grabs* **Jimmy**'*s hat and umbrella. Places hat on mother's head and umbrella in her arms.*) There you are, you're a judge. Now sum up and pass judgment.

Mrs Bryant   I'd put him in prison for life.

Frank   You gotta sum up though. Blust, you just can't stick a man in prison and say nothing.

Mrs Bryant   Goodbye, I'd say.

Beatie   Come on Mother, speak up. Anybody can say 'go to prison', but *you* want to be a judge. Well, you show a judge's understanding. Talk! Come on Mother, talk!

Everyone leans forward eagerly to hear mother talk. She looks startled and speechless.

Mrs Bryant   Well I – I – yes I – well I – Oh, don't be so soft.

Frank   The mighty head is silent.

Beatie   Well yes, she would be wouldn't she.

Mrs Bryant   What do you mean, I would be? You don't expect me to know what they say in courts do you? I aren't no judge.

Beatie   Then why do you sit and pass judgment on people? If someone do something wrong you don't stop and think why. No discussin', no questions, just – (*Snap of fingers.*) Off with his head. I mean look at Father getting less money. I don't see the family sittin' together and discussin' it. It's a problem! But which of you said it concerns you?

Mrs Bryant   Nor don't it concern them. I aren't hevin' people mix in my matters.

Beatie   But they aren't just people – they're your family for hell's sake!

Mrs Bryant   No matters, I aren't hevin' it!

Beatie   But Mother I –

Mrs Bryant   Now shut you up Beatie Bryant and leave it alone. I shall talk when I hev to and I never shall do, so there!

Beatie   You're so stubborn.

Mrs Bryant   So you keep saying.

Mr Bryant *enters, he is clean and dressed in blue pin-striped suit.*

Mr Bryant   You brewed up yit?

Mrs Bryant (*jumping up and going to kitchen*)   Oh hell, yes – I forgot the tea look.

Mr Bryant   Well, now we're all waitin' on him.

Jenny   Don't look as if Susie's comin'.

Beatie   Stubborn cow!

Silence.

Jenny   Hev you seen Susie's television set yit?

Beatie   I seen it.

Frank   Did you know also that when they fist hed it they took it up to bed wi' them and lay in bed wi' a dish of chocolate biscuits?

Pearl   But now they don't bother – they say they've had it a year now and all the old programmes they saw in the beginning they're seein' again.

Mrs Bryant (*entering with tea*)   Brew's up!

Beatie   Oh, for Christ's sake let's stop gossiping.

Pearl   I aren't gossiping. I'm making an intelligent observation about the state of television, now then.

Mr Bryant   What's up wi' you now?

Beatie   You weren't doin' nothin' o' the sort – you was gossiping.

Pearl   Well that's a heap sight better'n quotin' all the time.

Beatie   I don't quote all the time, I just tell you what Ronnie say.

Frank   Take it easy gal – he's comin' soon – don't need to go all jumpin' an' frantic.

Beatie   Listen! Let me set you a problem.

Jimmy   Here we go.

Beatie   While we're waitin' for him I'll set you a moral problem. You know what a moral problem is? It's a problem about right and wrong. I'll get you buggers thinking if it's the last thing I do. Now listen. There are four huts –

Frank   What?

Beatie   Huts. You know – them little things you live in. Now there are two huts on one side of a stream and two huts on the other side. On one side live a girl in one hut and a wise man in the other. On the other side live Tom in one hut and Archie in the other. Also there's a ferryman what run a boat across the river. Now – listen, concentrate – the girl loves Archie but Archie don't love the girl. And Tom love the girl but the girl don't go much on Tom.

Jimmy   Poor bugger.

Beatie   One day the girl hears that Archie – who don't love her, remember – is going to America, so she decides to try once more to persuade him to take her with him. So listen what she do. She go to the ferryman and ask him to take her across. The ferryman say, I will, but you must take off all your clothes.

Mrs Bryant   Well, whatever do he wanna ask that for?

Beatie   It don't matters why – he do! Now the girl doesn't know what to do so she ask the wise man for advice, and he say, you must do what you think best.

Frank   Well that weren't much advice was it!

Beatie   No matters – he give it. So the girl thinks about it and being so in love she decides to strip.

Pearl   Oh I say!

Mr Bryant   Well, this is a rum ole story ent it?

Beatie   Shut up Father and listen. Now, er – where was I?

Mr Bryant   She was strippin'.

Beatie   Oh yes! So, the girl strips and the ferryman takes her over – he don't touch her or nothing – just takes her over and she rushes to Archie's hut to implore him to take her with him and to declare her love again. Now Archie promises to take her with him and so she sleeps with him the night. But when she wake up in the morning he've gone. She's left alone. So she go across to Tom and explain her plight and ask for help. But soon ever he knowed what she've done, he chuck her out see? So there she is. Poor little gal. Left alone with no clothes and no friends and no hope of staying alive. Now – this is the question, think about it, don't answer quick – who is the person most responsible for her plight?

Jimmy   Well, can't she get back?

Beatie   No, she can't do anything. She's finished. She've hed it! Now, who's to blame?

There is a general air of thought for a moment and **Beatie** *looks triumphant and pleased with herself.*

Mrs Bryant   Be you a-drinkin' on your tea look. Don't you worry about no naked gals. The gal won't get cold but the tea will.

Pearl   Well I say the girl's most responsible.

Beatie   Why?

Pearl   Well, she made the choice didn't she?

Frank   Yes, but the old ferryman made her take off her clothes.

Pearl   But she didn't hev to.

Frank   Blust woman, she were in love!

Beatie   Good ole Frank.

Jenny   Hell if I know.

Beatie   Jimmy?

Jimmy   Don't ask me gal – I follow decisions, I aren't makin' none.

Beatie   Father?

Mr Bryant   I don't know what you're on about.

Beatie   Mother?

Mrs Bryant   Drink you your tea gal – never you mind what I think.

This is what they're waiting for.

Pearl   Well – what do Ronnie say?

Beatie   He say the gal is responsible only for makin' the decision to strip off and go across and that she do that because she's in love. After that she's the victim of two phoney men – one who don't love her but take advantage of her and one who say he love her but don't love her enough to help her, and that the man who say he love her but don't do nothin' to help her is most responsible because he were the last one she could turn to.

Jenny   He've got it all worked out then!

Beatie (*jumping on a chair thrusting her fist into the air like Ronnie, and glorying in what is the beginning of a hysteric outburst of his quotes*) 'No one do that bad that you can't forgive them.'

Pearl   He's sure of himself then?

Beatie   'We can't be sure of everything but certain basic things we must be sure about or we'll die.'

Frank   He think everyone is gonna listen then?

Beatie · 'People *must* listen. It's no good talking to the converted. *Everyone* must argue and think or they will stagnate and rot and the rot will spread.'

Jenny   Hark at that then.

Beatie (*her strange excitement growing; she has a quote for everything*) 'If wanting the best things in life means being a snob then glory hallelujah I'm a snob. But I'm not a snob Beatie, I just believe in human dignity and tolerance and cooperation and equality and –'

Jimmy (*jumping up in terror*)   He's a communist!

Beatie   'I'm a socialist!'

There is a knock on the front door.

Beatie (*jumping down joyously as though her excited quotes have been leading to this one moment*)   He's here, he's here! (*But at the door it is the postman, from whom she takes a letter and a parcel.*) Oh, the silly fool, the fool. Trust him to write a letter on the day he's coming. Parcel for you Mother.

Pearl   Oh, that'll be your dress from the club.

Mrs Bryant   What dress is this then? I didn't ask for no dress from the club.

Pearl   Yes you did, you did ask me, didn't she ask me Frank? Why, we were looking through the book together Mother.

Mrs Bryant   No matters what we was doin' together I aren't hevin' it.

Pearl   But Mother you distinctly –

Mrs Bryant   I aren't hevin' it so there now!

Beatie *has read the letter – the contents stun her. She cannot move. She stares around speechlessly at everyone.*

Mrs Bryant   Well, what's the matter wi' you gal? Let's have a read. (*Takes letter and reads contents in a dead flat but loud voice – as though it were a proclamation.*) 'My dear Beatie. It wouldn't really work would it? My ideas about handing on a new kind of life are quite useless and romantic if I'm really honest. If I were a healthy human being it might have been all right but most of us intellectuals are pretty sick and neurotic – as you have often observed – and we couldn't build a world even if we were given the reins of government – not yet any rate. I don't blame you for being stubborn, I don't blame you for ignoring every suggestion I ever made – I only blame myself for encouraging you to believe we could make a go of it and now two weeks of your not being here has given me the cowardly chance to think about it and decide and I –'

Beatie (*snatching letter*)   Shut up!

Mrs Bryant   Oh – so we know now do we?

Mr Bryant   What's this then – ent he comin'?

Mrs Bryant   Yes, we know now.

Mr Bryant   Ent he comin' I ask?

Beatie   *No he ent comin'.*

An awful silence ensues. Everyone looks uncomfortable.

Jenny (*softly*)   Well blust gal, didn't you know this was going to happen?

Beatie *shakes her head.*

Mrs Bryant   So *we're* stubborn are we?

Jenny   Shut you up Mother, the girl's upset.

Mrs Bryant   Well I can see that, I can see that, he ent coming, I can see that, and we're here like bloody fools, I can see that.

Pearl   Well did you quarrel all that much Beatie?

Beatie (*as if discovering this for the first time*)   He always wanted me to help him but I never could. Once he tried to teach me to type but soon ever I made a mistake I'd give up. I'd give up every time! I couldn't bear making mistakes. I don't know why, but I couldn't bear making mistakes.

Mrs Bryant   Oh – so we're hearin' the other side o' the story now are we?

Beatie   He used to suggest I start to copy real objects on to my paintings instead of only abstracts and I never took heed.

Mrs Bryant   Oh, so you never took heed.

Jenny   Shut you up I say.

Beatie   He gimme a book sometimes and I never bothered to read it.

Frank (*not maliciously*)   What about all this discussion we heard of?

Beatie   I *never* discussed things. He used to beg me to discuss things but I never saw the point on it.

Pearl   And he got riled because o' that?

Beatie (*trying to understand*)   I didn't have any patience.

Mrs Bryant   Now it's coming out.

Beatie   I couldn't help him – I never knew patience. Once he looked at me with terrified eyes and said, 'We've been together for three years but you don't know who I am or what I'm trying to say – and you don't care do you?'

Mrs Bryant   And there she was tellin' me.

Beatie   I never knew what he wanted – I didn't think it mattered.

Mr Bryant   And there she was gettin' us to solve the moral problem and now we know she didn't even do it herself. That's a rum 'un, ent it?

Mrs Bryant   The apple don't fall far from the tree – that it don't.

Beatie (*wearily*)   So you're proud on it? You sit there smug and you're proud that a daughter of yours wasn't able to help her boyfriend? Look at you. All of you. You can't say anything. You can't even help your own flesh and blood. Your daughter's bin ditched. It's your problem as well isn't it? I'm part of your family aren't I? Well, help me then! Give me words of comfort! Talk to me – for God's sake, someone talk to me. (*She cries at last.*)

Mr Bryant   Well, what do we do now?

Mrs Bryant   We sit down and we eat that's what we do now.

Jenny   Don't be soft Mother, we can't leave the girl crying like that.

Mrs Bryant   Well, blust, 'tent my fault she's cryin'. I did what I could – I prepared all this food, I'd've treated him as my own son if he'd come but he hevn't! We got a whole family gathering specially to greet him, all on us look, but he hevn't come. So what am I supposed to do?

Beatie   My God, Mother, I hate you – the only thing I ever wanted and I weren't able to keep him, I didn't know how. I hate you, I hate . . .

Mrs Bryant *slaps* **Beatie***'s face. Everyone is a little shocked at this harsh treatment.*

Mrs Bryant   There! I hed enough!

Mr Bryant   Well what d'you wanna do that for?

Mrs Bryant   I hed enough. All this time she've bin home she've bin tellin' me I didn't do this and I didn't do that and I hevn't understood half what she've said and I've hed enough. She talk about bein' part o' the family but she've never lived at home since she've left school look. Then she go away from here and fill her head wi' high-class squit and then it turn out she don't understand any on it herself. It turn out she do just the same things she say I do. (*Into* **Beatie***'s face.*) Well, am I right gal? I'm right ent I? When you tell me I was stubborn, what you mean was that *he* told you *you* was stubborn – eh? When you tell me I don't understand you mean *you* don't understand isn't it? When you tell me I don't make no effort you mean *you* don't make no effort. Well, what you blaming me for? Blaming me all the time! I haven't bin responsible for you since you left home – you bin on your own. She think I like it, she do! Thinks I like it being cooped up in this house all day. Well I'm telling you my gal – I don't! There! And if I had a chance to be away working somewhere the whole lot on you's could go to hell – the lot on you's. All right so I am a bloody fool – all right! So I know it! A whole two weeks I've bin told it. Well, so then I can't help you my gal, no that I can't, and you get used to that once and for all.

Beatie   No you can't Mother, I know you can't.

Mrs Bryant   I suppose doin' all those things for him weren't enough. I suppose he weren't satisfied wi' goodness only.

Beatie   Oh, what's the use.

Mrs Bryant   Well, don't you sit there an' sigh gal like you was Lady Nevershit. I ask you something. Answer me. You do the talking then. Go on – you say you know something we don't so *you* do the talking. Talk – go on, talk gal.

Beatie (*despairingly*)   I can't Mother, you're right – the apple don't fall far from the tree do it? You're right, I'm like you. Stubborn, empty, wi' no tools for livin'. I got no roots in nothing. I come from a family o' farm labourers yet I ent got no roots – just like town people – just a mass o' nothin'.

Frank   Roots, gal? What do you mean, roots?

Beatie (*impatiently*)   Roots, roots, roots! Christ, Frankie, you're in the fields all day, you should know about growing things. Roots! The things you come from, the things that feed you. The things that make you proud of yourself – roots!

Mr Bryant   You got a family ent you?

Beatie   I am not talking about family roots – I mean – the – I mean – Look! Ever since it begun the world's bin growin' hasn't it? Things hev happened, things have bin discovered, people have bin thinking and improving and inventing but what do we know about it all?

Jimmy   What is she on about?

Beatie (*various interjections*)   What do you mean, what am I on about? I'm talking! Listen to me! I'm tellin' you that the world's bin growing for two thousand years and we hevn't noticed it. I'm telling you that we don't know what we are or where we come from. I'm telling you something's cut us off from the beginning. I'm telling you we've got no roots. Blimey Joe! We've all got large allotments, we all grow things around us so we should know about roots. You know how to keep your flowers alive don't you Mother? Jimmy – you know how to keep the roots of your veges strong and healthy. It's not only the corn that need strong roots, you know, it's us too. But what've we got? Go on, tell me, what've we got? We don't know where we push up from and we don't bother neither.

Pearl   Well, I aren't grumbling.

Beatie   You say you aren't – oh yes, you say so, but look at you. What've you done since you come in? Hev you said anythin'? I mean really said or done anything to show you're alive? Alive! Blust, what do it mean? Do you know what it mean? Any of you? Shall I tell you what Susie said when I went and saw her? She say she don't care if that ole atom bomb drop and she die – that's what she say. And you know why she say it? I'll tell you why, because if she had to care she'd have to do something about it and she find *that* too much effort. Yes she do. She can't be bothered – she's too bored with it all. That's what we all are – we're all too bored.

Mrs Bryant   Blust woman – bored you say, bored? You say Susie's bored, with a radio and television an' that? I go t'hell if she's bored!

Beatie   Oh yes, we turn on a radio or a TV set maybe, or
we go to the pictures – if them's love stories or gangsters – but
isn't that the easiest way out? Anything so long as we don't
have to make an effort. Well, am I right? You know I'm right.
Education ent only books and music – it's asking questions, all
the time. There are millions of us, all over the country, and no
one, not one of us, is asking questions, we're all taking the
easiest way out. Everyone I ever worked with took the easiest
way out. We don't fight for anything, we're so mentally lazy
we might as well be dead. Blust, we are dead! And you know
what Ronnie say sometimes? He say it serves us right! That's
what he say – it's our own bloody fault!

Jimmy   So that's us summed up then – so we know where *we*
are then!

Mrs Bryant   Well if he don't reckon we count nor nothin',
then it's as well he didn't come. There! It's as well he didn't
come.

Beatie   Oh, *he* thinks we count all right – living in mystic
communion with nature. Living in mystic bloody communion
with nature (*indeed*). But us count? Count Mother? I wonder.
Do we? Do you think we really count? You don' wanna take
any notice of what them ole papers say about the workers
bein' all-important these days – that's all squit! 'Cos we aren't.
Do you think when the really talented people in the country
get to work they get to work for us? Hell if they do! Do you
think they don't know we 'ont make the effort? The 'I'll wait
for you in the heavens blue' writers don't write thinkin' we can
understand, nor the painters don't paint expecting us to be
interested – that they don't, nor don't the composers give out
music thinking we can appreciate it. 'Blust,' they say, 'the
masses is too stupid for us to come down to them. Blust,' they
say, 'if they don't make no effort why should we bother?' So
you know who come along? The slop singers and the pop
writers and the film makers and women's magazines and the
Sunday papers and the picture-strip love stories – that's who
come along, and you don't have to make no effort for them, it

come easy. 'We know where the money lie,' they say, 'hell we do! The workers've got it so let's give them what they want. If they want slop songs and film idols we'll give 'em that then. If they want words of one syllable, we'll give 'em that then. If they want the third-rate, *blust*! We'll give 'em *that* then. Anything's good enough for them 'cos they don't ask for no more!' The whole stinkin' commercial world insults us and we don't care a damn. Well, Ronnie's right – it's our own bloody fault. We want the third-rate – we got it! We got it! We got it! We . . .

Suddenly **Beatie** *stops as if listening to herself. She pauses, turns with an ecstatic smile on her face –*

D'you hear that? D'you hear it? Did you listen to me? I'm talking. Jenny, Frankie, Mother – I'm not quoting no more.

Mrs Bryant (*getting up to sit at table*)   Oh hell, I hed enough of her – let her talk a while she'll soon get fed up.

The others join her at the table and proceed to eat and murmur.

Beatie   Listen to me someone. (*As though a vision were revealed to her.*) God in heaven, *Ronnie*! It does work, it's happening to me, I can feel it's happening, I'm beginning, on my own two feet – I'm beginning . . .

The murmur of the family sitting down to eat grows as **Beatie**'s *last cry is heard. Whatever she will do they will continue to live as before. As* **Beatie** *stands alone, articulate at last –*

The curtain falls.

Music

'I'll wait for you in the heavens blue' (pages 39–40)

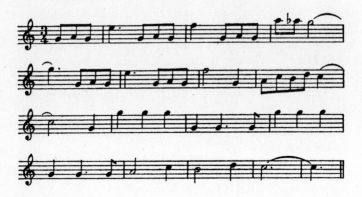

Bloomsbury Methuen Drama Modern Plays

include work by

Bola Agbaje
Edward Albee
Davey Anderson
Jean Anouilh
John Arden
Peter Barnes
Sebastian Barry
Alistair Beaton
Brendan Behan
Edward Bond
William Boyd
Bertolt Brecht
Howard Brenton
Amelia Bullmore
Anthony Burgess
Leo Butler
Jim Cartwright
Lolita Chakrabarti
Caryl Churchill
Lucinda Coxon
Curious Directive
Nick Darke
Shelagh Delaney
Ishy Din
Claire Dowie
David Edgar
David Eldridge
Dario Fo
Michael Frayn
John Godber
Paul Godfrey
James Graham
David Greig
John Guare
Mark Haddon
Peter Handke
David Harrower
Jonathan Harvey
Iain Heggie

Robert Holman
Caroline Horton
Terry Johnson
Sarah Kane
Barrie Keeffe
Doug Lucie
Anders Lustgarten
David Mamet
Patrick Marber
Martin McDonagh
Arthur Miller
D. C. Moore
Tom Murphy
Phyllis Nagy
Anthony Neilson
Peter Nichols
Joe Orton
Joe Penhall
Luigi Pirandello
Stephen Poliakoff
Lucy Prebble
Peter Quilter
Mark Ravenhill
Philip Ridley
Willy Russell
Jean-Paul Sartre
Sam Shepard
Martin Sherman
Wole Soyinka
Simon Stephens
Peter Straughan
Kate Tempest
Theatre Workshop
Judy Upton
Timberlake Wertenbaker
Roy Williams
Snoo Wilson
Frances Ya-Chu Cowhig
Benjamin Zephaniah

For a complete catalogue
of Bloomsbury Methuen Drama
titles write to:

Bloomsbury Methuen Drama
Bloomsbury Publishing Plc
50 Bedford Square
London WC1B 3DP

or you can visit our website at:
www.bloomsbury.com/drama